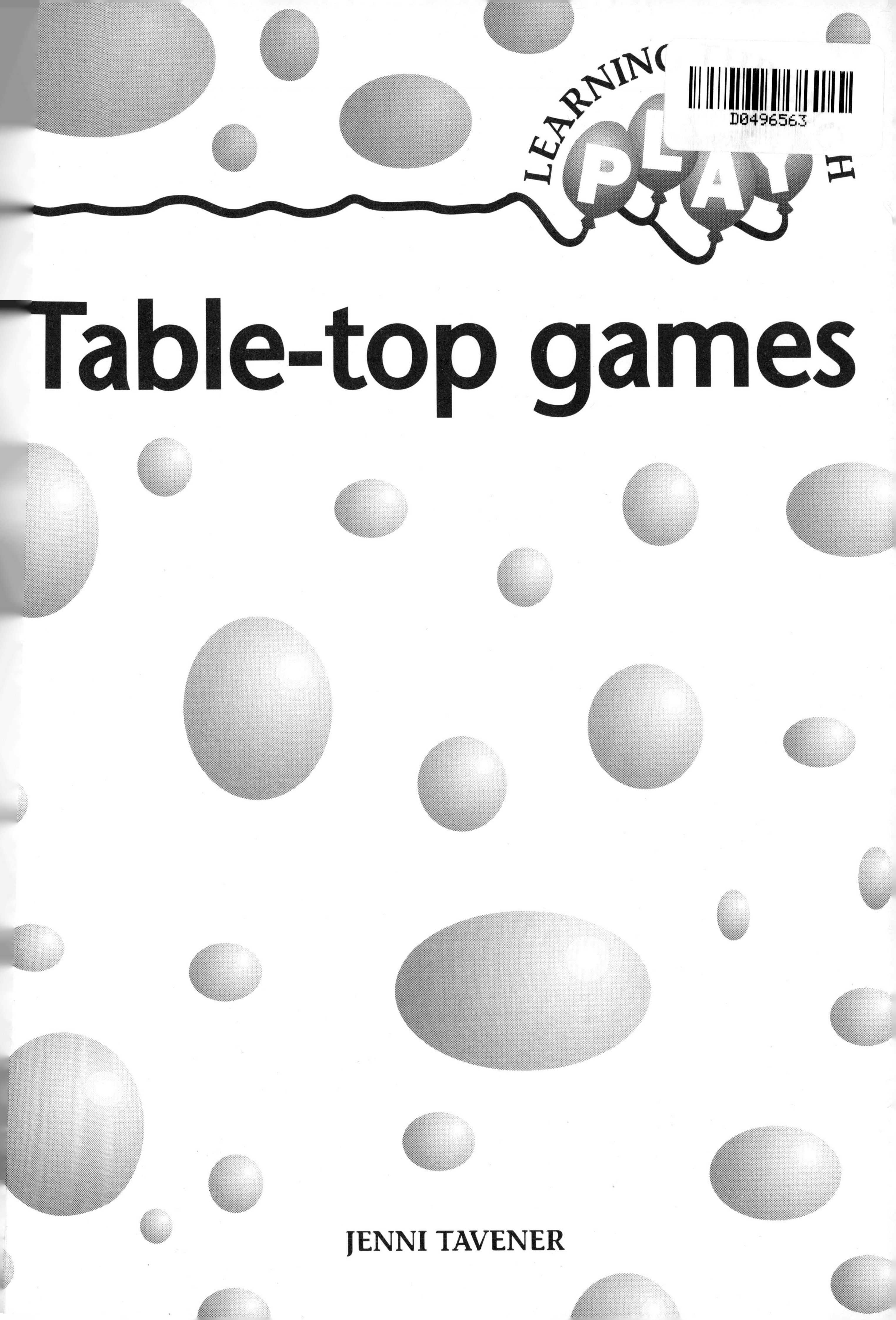

Table-top games
JENNI TAVENER

Published by Scholastic Ltd,
Villiers House,
Clarendon Avenue,
Leamington Spa,
Warwickshire CV32 5PR

1 2 3 4 5 6 7 8 9 8 9 0 1 2 3 4 5 6 7

Author
Jenni Tavener

Editor
Clare Gallaher

Assistant Editor
Lesley Sudlow

Series designer
Lynne Joesbury

Designer
Rachel Warner

Illustrations
Denise Elliot
(Simon Girling & Associates)

Cover photograph
Martyn Chillmaid

For Chris

Designed using Adobe Pagemaker

British Library Cataloguing-in-Publication Data
A catalogue record for this book is available from the British Library.

ISBN 0-590-53723-7

CONTENTS

CHAPTER 4: KNOWLEDGE AND UNDERSTANDING OF THE WORLD

CHAPTER 5: PHYSICAL DEVELOPMENT

CHAPTER 6: CREATIVE DEVELOPMENT

PHOTOCOPIABLES

INTRODUCTION

Using games

Table-top games provide a valuable role for developing children's interest and learning. Children love games and are more likely to recall knowledge and skills when they are acquired through enjoyable learning situations. Table-top games can cover a wide range of curricular areas, as well as providing a sound resource for promoting important issues such as taking turns, co-operation, team work and sharing.

This book offers practitioners working in schools and nurseries an extensive range of original games, tried and tested for particular use with early years children. It also provides a wide range of ideas for children to design, create or make their own games.

Learning through play

Games provide a host of educational opportunities through play. The table-top games or follow-up activities in this book can be used to offer structured and 'free' play in a comfortable learning environment. Games can be used as a valuable resource for the development of a positive self-image. As children begin to master the games, it is hoped that they will gain confidence and as a result improve their self-concepts.

The games in this book are designed to be flexible and to cater for the needs of individual children. The variety of games has also been carefully planned to offer a wide range of approaches to stimulate learning through play.

How to use this book

The chapters in this book are organised into the six Areas of Learning for the under-fives that have been identified by the School Curriculum and Assessment Authority (SCAA) in the *Desirable Outcomes for Children's Learning*. These are Language and Literacy (Chapter 1), Mathematics (Chapter 2), Personal and Social Development (Chapter 3), Knowledge and Understanding of the World (Chapter 4), Physical Development

(Chapter 5) and Creative Development (Chapter 6). Each chapter offers eight table-top game ideas which have been designed to help develop the children's skills across these six areas and to stimulate the children's interest and motivation to learn through play.

Each activity identifies the main learning objective of the game. It also gives an indication of the group size or number of players suitable for the game. All the resources necessary to make and/or play the games are clearly listed under the heading 'What you need'. A section entitled 'Setting up' provides useful information for the practitioner about how to organise the materials or how to involve the children in preparing for the game. Then each game is described, stage by stage, in 'How to play'. Suggestions for questions to ask the children during or after the game are also provided.

All the games can be easily adapted or extended to suit the needs of individual children, and suggestions to do this are provided under the headings 'For younger children' or 'For older children'. Follow-up activities provide a range of ideas for developing work in different subjects which link with the theme of the game.

There are six photocopiable pages at the end of the book. Four of these provide games which can be used to help reinforce skills such as pattern matching, sorting and sequencing, handling money and counting on. Two further photocopiable pages provide pictures to assist practitioners or to enable the children to create games.

Equipment, storage and organisation

Almost all of the games can be played over and over again. To protect the games from becoming lost or damaged, it is a good idea to store them carefully. The games can then be kept to use whenever the need arises. Most of the board games have been designed so that they can be stored in A3 or A4 size pocket folders. Where games require very large game boards

(A1 size), it is suggested that a 'game sheet' be made from fabric. These games can then be easily folded and, once again, stored in A3 or A4 pocket folders.

All of the accessories for each game, such as dice and counters, should be stored with the game board or game sheet inside the folder. Label each folder with the name of the game, the appropriate page number from this *Table-top games* book and the Area of Learning to which the game relates.

As time goes by, you may gradually build up a collection of 'game folders'. These can then be kept within labelled box files or sturdy containers along with *Table-top games* for reference. Where appropriate, it is suggested that the game boards, game cards, photocopiable games and so on are covered in transparent self-adhesive plastic film. This comes in various sizes, and it would be a good idea to set aside some in two different sizes (A4 and A3) for use as soon as a game is made in order to keep it fresh and clean in appearance, and to protect it from tearing during play.

When games are drawn onto fabric, it is advisable to use a permanent marker, or suitable fabric crayons or paints so that they can be washed if the need arises.

Commercial dice are not essential. Suitable dice can be easily made by the practitioner or the children using old wooden or plastic bricks and sticky labels. Alternative suggestions include using 'spinners' or placing number cards, balls or blocks inside a 'lucky dip' bag.

Planning and preparation

Many of the games in this book require some of the resources to be made in advance by the practitioner or by the children. Make sure all the materials that you require are readily available. In some cases, it is suggested that the practitioner makes an example game board to show the children. It is important that this is done before introducing the activity to them, as it will give you an opportunity to assess how to organise and plan the activity to achieve the best results.

Observation and assessment

It is extremely important to be sensitive towards observing or assessing the children while they are playing games. When and how observations and assessments are made should be considered very carefully. Children should feel totally at ease while playing their games, and the atmosphere created should be one of promoting confidence and self-esteem. They can become very self-conscious if they feel that they are being watched, and this feeling can even turn into one of 'worry' if they see that somebody might be writing notes about them – Did I do that wrong? What happens if I don't know what to do next?

For all these reasons, embarking on observations and assessments will need your utmost professional judgement. Much information can be acquired by playing the games with the children, talking to them about the game and by asking open-ended questions. In a relaxed situation such as this, the children will feel at ease and are more likely to achieve their true potential. If written assessments are necessary, try to record your findings immediately, after the game is over, away from the view of the children. If this is not possible or the assessment requires 'on task' written observations, try to sit within sight and earshot but at a discreet distance.

If appropriate, explain to the children what you are doing, making sure it is put across as something positive. Then provide them with follow-up information – 'I liked the way you took turns', 'I noticed that you shared nicely', 'Can I join you during the next game?' and so on.

Links with home

Some children may have had many opportunities to play games at home, while other children may rarely play games at home. Try involving parents and carers as much as possible with the games and activities that you organise. They will then become aware of the interest and learning which takes place during these games, and will hopefully support the work at home by playing more games with their children.

Many nurseries and schools send books home for the children to share with their parents. How about sending a game home occasionally? Invite parents in to play some of the games with the children. Take photographs of the children while they are involved in a game. Display a few examples of the games alongside the photographs for the parents to see when they bring or collect their children. Encourage the children to explain to their parents how they played the game. Develop as much communication as possible between home and your group, as this leads to a greater awareness and understanding of the children's needs and interests.

The adult's role

The role of the adult is very important and should change according to the situation. In some cases it may be necessary to play the game with the children, for example when introducing a new game or as a form of encouragement to children who are unfamiliar with playing games. At other times, it may be best to leave a group of children to play independently without any adult intervention. These situations will help the children to understand the necessity of teamwork, co-operation and fair play.

There are also likely to be circumstances when the adult's role means simply setting up the game, reminding the children of the rules and instructions, and then becoming an interested observer. Being available to ask and answer questions is important, as long as this does not interfere with the flow of the game or distract the children's attention.

Questions that you ask the children during the course of an activity (the section headed 'Questions to ask' provides suggestions) will depend upon your personal knowledge of the children or the skills you are aiming to develop. For example, you may wish to initiate descriptive language by using open-ended questions; or to encourage forward thinking you may decide to ask questions such as 'In which direction should you move your counter to reach the...?' or 'What number do you need to throw to reach the...?'

As the children become more adept at playing the games, the adult's role will change to accommodate this, for example by inviting the children to help extend the games or adapt the instructions, or by introducing new challenges, such as using dice with higher numbers or using two dice for addition and subtraction.

TABLE-TOP GAMES

LANGUAGE AND LITERACY

KNOWLEDGE AND UNDERSTANDING OF THE WORLD

MATHEMATICS

PHYSICAL DEVELOPMENT

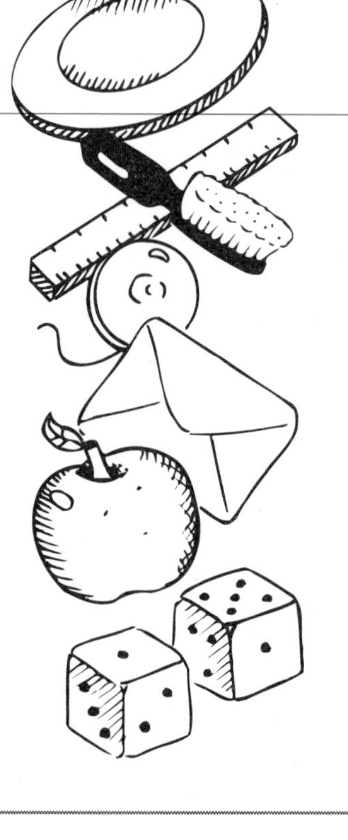

PERSONAL AND SOCIAL DEVELOPMENT

CREATIVE DEVELOPMENT

The activities in this chapter will develop children's language and literacy skills, including talking and listening skills, letter and sound recognition and descriptive language. Games such as 'Treasure island' can be used to inspire storytelling skills and creative imagination. Other games, such as the 'Rhyming words game' can be used to stimulate an interest in rhyming words.

LISTEN TO THE SOUNDS

Learning objective
To encourage listening skills and to develop vocabulary to describe experiences.

Group size
Small group.

What you need
A cassette recorder, cassette, five musical instruments (or five objects which can be used to make a noise – paper to rustle, a container of water to shake, a tin to tap and so on) felt-tipped pens, card or paper.

Setting up
Tape-record a series of five different noises. Write a name card for each child. Place the five instruments (or objects) on the table, and invite the children to have fun making different sounds. Before the game starts, provide each child with their own name card.

How to play
The players listen to the tape recording of the first sound. They then place their name card beside the instrument (or object) which they think made the first sound. When all the name cards are in place, show the children which instrument (or object) made the sound, and how it was made.

This process is repeated with the other four sounds. Play can be for fun, or a winner can be found by recording who has the highest number of correct answers out of five.

Questions to ask
How would you describe these sounds? Do you have any favourite sounds? Why? Are there any noises that you dislike? Why?

For younger children
Let the children experiment with the instruments (or objects) to make a variety of sounds. Encourage them to listen carefully and to differentiate between loud and quiet sounds.

For older children
Can they think of descriptive words to explain the different sounds? Invite them to make up 'new' words.

Follow-up activities
- Record a series of sounds commonly heard in the group's room.
- Talk about important sounds, such as a fire-alarm, car horn, bicycle bell.
- Organise a 'sound table' for interactive play.

WHAT AM I?

Learning objective
To develop observation skills and descriptive language, and to encourage children to listen attentively.

Group size
Four to six players.

What you need

Strips of card (long enough to fit around a child's head), adhesive tape, small pictures of familiar animals.

Setting up

Use the card strips to make a headband for each child. Ask the children to wear their headbands, while you secure a picture of an animal to the back of each band (make sure the children do not see the animal that they are wearing). Then ask them to sit in a circle around the table so that everyone can see each other clearly.

How to play

The first player twists her headband around so her animal picture can be seen. The children in the circle should take it in turn to describe one or two features associated with the animal on the headband of the first player – 'You have fur', 'You have a long tail', 'You are small', 'You have whiskers', for example. When everybody has given a description the first player should then guess what animal she is. If correct, she can remove her headband.

If she is wrong, she can either remove her headband to find out what animal she is, or keep the headband on and wait for another go. The second player should then twist her headband around to reveal her animal picture for the rest of the group to describe. This process is repeated until every child has had a turn at guessing 'what they are'.

Questions to ask

Assist the children giving the descriptions by asking questions to help their observations: is the animal big or small? Has it got feathers, fur, scales or skin? Help the children to make use of their background knowledge of each animal by asking questions such as: what noise does the animal make? What does it eat?
Does it live on land or in water?

For younger children

Place a second set of identical pictures face up, in the centre of the table. The players can then listen to the descriptions and select which one of the animals they think they are.

Follow-up activities
- Paint a picture of a pet or favourite animal.
- Make animal masks for mime and drama.
- Set up a display of books about animals.

For older children

Include more unusual animals such as minibeasts, zoo animals or underwater creatures.

ALPHABET PASS THE PARCEL

Learning objective
To help children to recognise letters of the alphabet and to practise the sounds which correspond with them.

Group size
Three to six players.

What you need

One copy of photocopiable page 59, cassette recorder, cassette with music of your choice, a box with easy-to-open lid, a sheet of card (approx. 60cm × 60cm), 26 small sheets of brightly coloured paper (approx. 10cm × 10cm), 26 small pieces of card (approx. 10cm × 10cm), PVA adhesive, felt-tipped pens, scissors, plastic film.

Setting up

To make the game board: Write the alphabet onto the 26 sheets of coloured paper and paste them onto the large sheet of card. Cover it in plastic film. (See diagram.)
To make the picture cards: Cut copies of the photocopiable sheet into the 26 individual pictures, mount them onto 26 small pieces of card and cover them in plastic film. Place the cards in a box.

Ask the children to sit around a table. Place the alphabet game board in the centre of the table and position the cassette recorder nearby.

How to play

Hand the box containing the pictures to the first child, and turn on the music. Tell the children to 'pass the parcel' around the table until the music stops.

When the music stops, the child holding the box then removes one or two of the pictures and matches them to the correct letters on the 'alphabet game board'. When the music begins, the box is passed around the group again. Play continues, 'pass the parcel' style, until all the pictures have been placed onto the game board.

Questions to ask

What letter does, say, 'apple' begin with? Can you find an 'a' on the game board? What sound does 'a' make? Can you think of any other word beginning with 'a'?

For younger children

Assist them in matching the pictures to the correct letter. Highlight the 'sounds' of the letters.

For older children

Encourage the children to recall the name and sound of each letter.

Follow-up activities
- Sing an 'abc' song.
- Paint an alphabet frieze.
- Play 'I spy...'.

THE NAME GAME

Learning objective
To help children to recognise and spell their own name, and to develop observation and recall skills.

Group size
Small group.

What you need
A selection of toys (three per child), gummed labels (or paper and adhesive tape), felt-tipped pen, a box or bag for each player (make sure it is big enough to fit three toys inside).

Setting up
Write each child's name on three separate labels and secure them to the base of three toys. Place all the toys on the table, and ask the children to sit or stand around the table. Provide each child with an empty box.

How to play
The first player picks up any toy, and turns it over so that everyone can see the name label on the base. If the name is her own she places the toy in her box. If the name is not hers, she should replace the toy on the table. The other players then take it in turns to repeat this process. The first child to recover all three toys labelled with her name is the winner.

Questions to ask
Amy picked up a toy with your name on it – can you remember which toy that was? What letter does this name begin with? What letter does your name begin with? This name is spelled 'T-i-m'; whose name is this? How do you spell your name?

For younger children
Write their first name only on the labels. Provide each child with a name card so that they can refer to it when identifying their name label.

For older children
Write the children's first name and surname on the label, or include a slightly different message on each of the three labels for the children to read, for example 'My name is Sophie', 'I am called Sophie', 'Sophie is my name'.

Follow-up activities
- Make a name badge to wear.
- Use a mirror to draw a self-portrait.
- Compile a mini 'passport' including name, age, birthday, address and a small photograph or drawing.

SHOE, WHERE ARE YOU?

Learning objective
To use descriptive language and to encourage observation and listening skills.

Group size
Small or large group.

What you need

A shoe bag (or box) for each child, a selection of clean boots and shoes such as a pair of football boots, wellington boots, baby booties, roller blades, children's shoes, slippers, ice-skates (with guards on), ballet shoes, hockey boots, climbing boots, sandals, flippers, stilettos and clogs.

Setting up

Ask the children to sit in a circle, and provide each child with a bag or box. Let each child select one shoe to 'hide' in their bag. Then ask one child (plus an adult helper if required) to sit in the centre of the circle, with all the matching shoes, that is, the partners to the shoes that the children have selected, plus some spare shoes.

How to play

One of the children in the circle describes the boot or shoe hidden in her bag, by stating two or three main features. For example: 'My shoe is blue. It is small. It is woolly.' The child in the centre should listen carefully to the description and then select the matching shoe to place inside the bag of the child in the circle who gave the description. The pair of shoes is then removed from the bag to see if it is a matching pair.

Let all the children take it in turn to be in the centre of the circle and to provide a description.

Questions to ask

What colour is the shoe in your bag? Would you wear it inside or outside? What does the sole of the shoe look like? Would it fit you, or would it be too big or small? What is the shoe made of?

For younger children

Make sure that the selection of shoes shows a range of very different features to enable fewer or less detailed descriptions to occur, and to make identification easier.

For older children

Include a selection of similar shoes in the circle, thus making it necessary for more detailed descriptions.

Follow-up activities
- Create a 'shoe shop' in the role-play area.
- Read rhymes and stories about shoes, such as 'Puss-in-boots', 'The Elves and the Shoemaker', 'The Slipper and the Rose', 'There was an Old Woman who lived in a Shoe'.
- Make a display of footprints.

TREASURE ISLAND

Learning objective
To use their imagination to create a game and to make up their own stories.

Group size
Two to four players.

What you need

A large sheet of paper or card (approx. 60cm × 60cm), felt-tipped pens or coloured pencils, a small box, some shiny 'jewels' or beads, a dice (with dots, numerals or words one to six), counters, PVA adhesive.

Setting up

Tell the children that they are going to help you to create a treasure island game. Draw the outline of an island onto a large sheet of paper or card. Glue a small box to the centre of the island, then draw a winding path leading from the box to the outside edge of the island. Divide the 'path' into approximately 20 to 30 sections, making sure that every third or fourth section is larger than the rest.

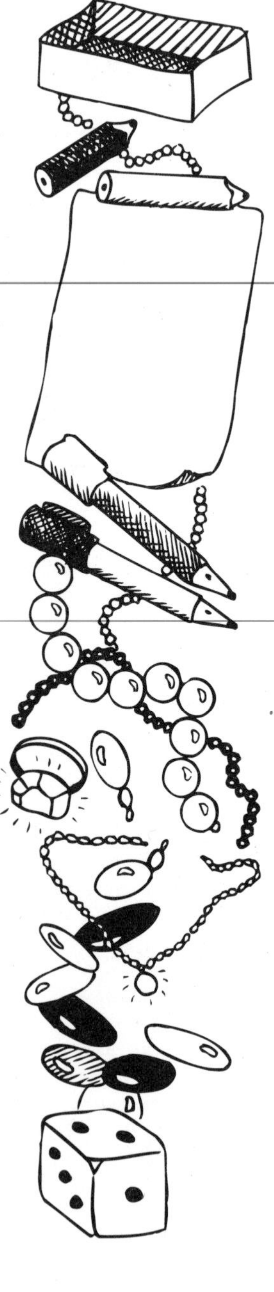

Invite the children to help transform the empty island into a 'treasure island' by thinking of obstacles to place in the path of treasure hunters. Let the children decide what type of features to include, for example a shark-infested lake, sinking sand or a lion's cave. Help them to draw their ideas inside the large spaces on the island. Then fill the box in the centre of the island with 'jewels'.

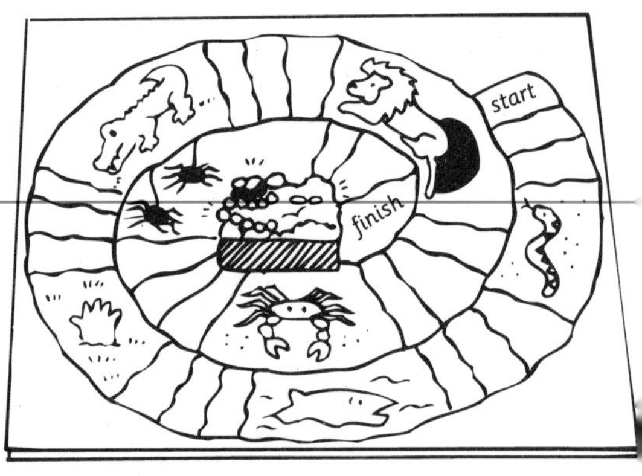

Place the treasure island game board on the table. Provide the players with counters and a dice.

How to play

The children take it in turns to throw the dice and move their counter accordingly along the 'treasure hunters' pathway'. If they land on one of the 'traps' they should move back two spaces. The winner is the first player to reach the treasure in the centre of the island.

Questions to ask

Imagine that you are on the island, how would you escape from the 'sinking sand' or 'lion's cave'? Who would you take with you to a treasure island? How would you get to the island? What would you do with the treasure?

For younger children

Use the treasure island game board to stimulate role play. Let the children use play people or small puppets to visit the island, tackle the obstacles and find the treasure.

For older children

Invite them to make up their own rules and instructions for the game. Encourage them to draw a picture story about a visit to the island. Explain that the story should have at least three pictures to show a beginning, middle and end. Some children may wish to include written captions to their story using emergent writing.

Follow-up activities
- Paint or collage a treasure map.
- Construct a treasure chest in three dimensions using boxes, shiny paper, 'jewels' and so on.
- Hide some 'treasure' indoors and play 'Hot and cold' – you are 'hot' if you are close to the treasure, 'cold' if not.

RHYMING WORDS GAME

Learning objective
To stimulate an interest in rhyming words.

Group size
Small group.

What you need

A collection of traditional or favourite rhymes, a collection of objects (or pictures) that rhyme (such as 'hook' and 'book'; 'cat' and 'mat'; 'boat' and 'coat'; 'pen' and 'hen'), a large sheet of paper or card, a dice (with dots, numerals or words one to six), a counter for each child.

Setting up

Create a simple game board by drawing a circle of approximately 20 'stepping stones' around the edge of the large sheet of paper or card. Place one half of the objects onto the 'stepping stones', and place their rhyming partners in the centre of the circle. For example, if the 'hook' is on a 'stepping stone', then the 'book' should be in the centre. (See diagram.)

Say some rhymes and poems with the children. Talk about the rhyming words.

objects (or pictures) on stepping stones

rhyming partners in centre

How to play

Each child places their counter on any empty 'stepping stone'. The first player throws the dice and moves accordingly, in any direction, around the 'stepping stones'. If she lands on a 'stone' containing an object, she should find its rhyming partner from the centre of the circle. She can then remove the pair of objects from the game board and keep them until the end of the game. The dice is then passed to the next player.

If players land on an empty 'stone', they do not collect any objects, and the dice is passed on straight away. This process is repeated, until the last two rhyming objects have been removed from the game board. The winner is the player who has collected the most objects.

Questions to ask

Can you think of other words which rhyme with this object? Which objects do we have on our game board that rhyme with 'look' and 'cook'?

For younger children

Assist the children in finding the rhyming partners by giving them two to choose from. For example: you have landed on a 'cat' – does this rhyme with a 'mat' or a 'coat'?

For older children

Label each object (or picture), so that the children can see the 'written pattern' of the rhyming words as well as hear the 'vocal pattern'.

Follow-up activities
- Make an interactive display of rhyming objects and place them into rhyming pairs.
- Collate a book of favourite poems and illustrate them.
- Play 'I spy something rhyming with...', but remember that more than one answer might be correct.

THE YELLOW BRICK ROAD

Learning objective
To recognise letters and letter sounds.

Group size
Two players or two teams.

What you need

Twelve yellow discs cut out of card (approx. 10cm × 10cm), a large cardboard box, a selection of ten to fifteen everyday objects (such as a cup, plate, brush, ruler, small saucepan, book, small wheel, envelope and so on), two dice (each with dots, numerals or words one to six), two small play people (or stuffed toys), a short version of L Frank Baum's *The Wizard of Oz* (Ladybird's edition, for example).

Setting up

Let the children help you construct a 'Wizard's palace' or 'Emerald City' from the cardboard box. Collect an assortment of everyday objects to place inside the 'palace'. Mark each yellow disc with a letter. Dress two play people to represent two of the characters in the story, choosing from the scarecrow, the tin man, the lion or Dorothy.

Read a short version of the story 'The Wizard of Oz' to the children. Place the yellow discs on the table in a line. Explain that these represent the yellow brick road. Place the 'palace' at one end of the road and a 'start' sign at the other.

selection of everyday objects

start f a b u c t e s a i

yellow card discs to represent yellow brick road

How to play

The first player throws one or both dice and moves one of the play people accordingly along the yellow brick road. If the disc on which the player lands displays a letter, say 'b', the player must correctly identify the sound of that letter (team or adult help may be needed here) and then collect any one object from the palace which begins with 'b'. If there is no object beginning with 'b' the player returns empty-handed. This process is repeated, each player (or team) taking turns until the palace is empty. The winner is the player (or team) with the most objects.

Questions to ask

What letters can you see along the yellow brick road? What sound does each letter make? What letter does that object begin with?

For younger children

Limit the letters on the yellow brick road to three or four that are familiar to them. Make sure that there are plenty of objects within the palace beginning with the letter sounds that you have chosen.

For older children

Include letter blends on the yellow brick road ('sh', 'br', 'pl' and so on), ensuring that the objects begin with your selection of blends (for example, 'ship', 'brick', 'plate'). Alternatively, use complete words or short instructional sentences (such as 'find a ball') on the yellow discs.

Follow-up activities
- Mime the stiff, jerky movements of the tin man or floppy movements of the scarecrow.
- Create a dressing-up area where they can act out their version of the story.
- Paint a scene from the story – the Emerald City, the palace, the rainbow and so on.

MATHEMATICS

This chapter provides ways of using games to encourage the children's mathematical skills. For instance, the activities 'Frog jumps' and 'Incy wincy' help to promote counting skills; 'Mary's garden' helps to develop an awareness of mathematical language. Activities are also provided to help to develop pattern matching, sequencing and handling money.

RING-A-RING O' ROSES

Learning objective
To develop skills in pattern matching.

Group size
Two players.

What you need

A copy of the photocopiable game sheet on page 60 for each child, felt-tipped pens or coloured pencils, a large plastic or wooden brick, gummed labels, a black marker pen.

Setting up

Create a patterned dice by copying the six patterns, illustrated on the photocopiable game sheet, onto six gummed labels. Place each label onto the six sides of a large brick. Ask a pair of children to sit together, and provide each child with a copy of the photocopiable game sheet and a felt-tipped pen or coloured pencil.

How to play

The first player throws the dice and then colours in a child on her game sheet which matches the pattern on the dice. The dice is then passed on to the next player. This process is repeated, the players taking turns to throw the dice and colouring in a child. If the child is already coloured in, the dice is passed on.

The winner is the first player to colour all the children on her sheet.

Questions to ask

How many different patterns can you see? How many children are there all together? How many children have stripy clothes? How many children have you coloured so far?

For younger children

Sit alongside the children and provide assistance when appropriate.

For older children

Provide the children with six different coloured felt-tipped pens or coloured pencils. Ask them to colour the pattern grid at the top of their page, making sure that each pattern is a different colour. During the game encourage the players to refer to their 'pattern grid' when colouring in the children on their game sheet.

Follow-up activities

- Provide each child with a swatch of plain cotton fabric (approx. 20cm × 20cm) to decorate with their own choice of pattern using fabric paints or crayons. Sew all the finished swatches together to create a unique cushion cover or wall-hanging.
- Look for patterns around the room.
- Go on a 'pattern hunt' outside. Look for patterns in brickwork, on the pavement, in flower-beds and so on.

THE BEAUTIFUL BUTTERFLY

Learning objective
To increase awareness of shape and colour.

Group size
One to four players.

What you need

Butterfly: A black marker pen, a sheet of white paper or fabric (approx. 1m × 1m).
Shapes: Card (in three different colours), scissors, plastic film.
Lucky dip: A selection of coloured bricks, balls or counters (the colours should relate to the coloured shapes), a small bag or box.

Setting up

Draw the outline of a butterfly onto a sheet of white paper or fabric using a black marker pen. Draw the outline of three large squares, triangles and circles (all approx. 10cm × 10cm) and three small squares, triangles and circles (all approx. 5cm × 5cm) inside the butterfly.

Cut a large square, triangle and circle (approx. 10cm × 10cm) and a small square triangle and circle (approx. 5cm × 5cm) from each sheet of coloured card, thus providing 18 shapes all together.

Put the selection of coloured bricks, balls or counters into a bag or box to create a 'lucky dip' bag. Place the butterfly sheet onto a low table and arrange the coloured shapes around the butterfly. Ask the children to stand around the table.

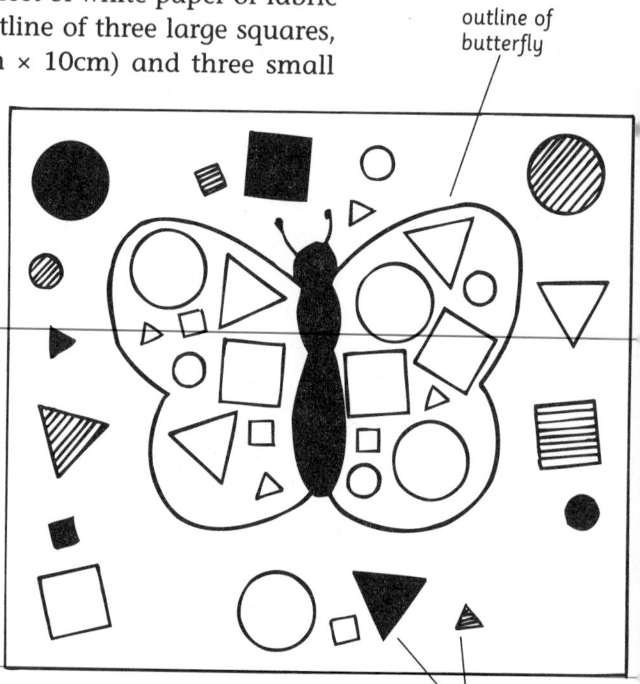

outline of butterfly

card shapes in different colours

How to play

The first child picks a coloured brick out of the lucky dip. If it is, for example, 'red' the child selects any 'red' shape from around the butterfly. Once a shape of the correct colour has been selected, it should be matched to the corresponding shape on the butterfly. This process is repeated, the children taking turns until the 'beautiful butterfly' is complete.

Questions to ask

What is the name of this shape? How many sides does it have? How many corners does it have? How many small shapes can you count? How many big shapes? How many triangles?

For younger children

Encourage the children to work in pairs to match the shapes and colours.

For older children

Five- or six-sided shapes, for example, could be introduced for matching, or more unusual colours could be used, such as gold and silver, or even patterns.

Follow-up activities
- Read a story which involves a 'beautiful butterfly', for example *The Very Hungry Caterpillar* by Eric Carle (Hamish Hamilton).
- Look at photographs or pictures of real butterflies and talk about the different patterns, colours and shapes on their wings.
- Go on a butterfly walk to observe butterflies in their natural environment.

MOUSEY, MOUSEY

Learning objective
Game 1: *To reinforce sequencing and sorting skills.*
Games 2 and 3: *To develop matching skills and pairing.*

Group size
Games 1 and 3: *Individuals and small groups.*
Game 2: *Two players.*

What you need

Card, scissors, plastic film, photocopiable page 61 (one copy for game 1 and two copies for game 2, all enlarged to A3 size, if possible).

Setting up

Game 1: Mount a copy of the photocopiable sheet onto card (or photocopy onto card) and cut it into the eight separate pictures. Cover them in plastic film.

Games 2 and 3: Repeat as for game 1, but use two copies of the photocopiable sheet to provide 16 separate picture cards.

Introduce sequencing by showing the children the eight cards used in game 1 in the correct order. Talk with them about why this order is correct. Ask the children to close their eyes or to look away briefly while you swap over two of the cards. Can they identify these two cards and put them back in the correct order? Let the children reinforce these skills by playing game 1.

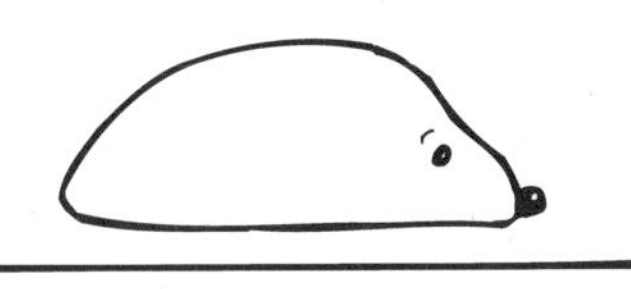

How to play

Game 1: Shuffle the eight cards and place them on the table, face up, in front of the child (or children). Ask them to look carefully at the pictures and to sort them into the correct order (see illustration).

Game 2: Shuffle all 16 cards and share them between the two children. Let them use the cards to play Snap.

Game 3: Shuffle all 16 cards and lay them face down on the table. Invite the children to take it in turns to turn over two cards to reveal two mouse pictures. If they match, that child can keep the pair of cards. If not, they should be replaced, face down, on the table. This process is repeated until all the cards have gone. The winner is the child with the most pairs.

Questions to ask

How many different pictures can you see? How many mice pictures have a nose, an eye, ears, a tail, whiskers, back legs, front legs?

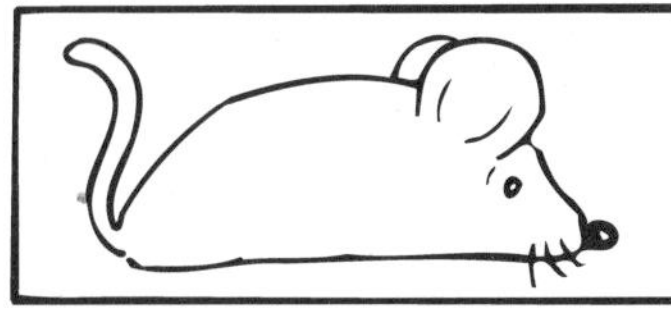

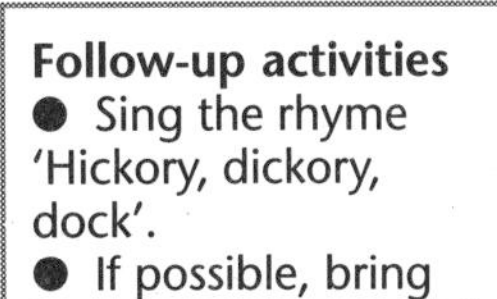

Follow-up activities
- Sing the rhyme 'Hickory, dickory, dock'.
- If possible, bring in a pet mouse, gerbil or hamster. Highlight the necessity to care for pets.
- Discuss the animal's needs, such as food, water, a clean home and gentle handling.

For younger children

Work alongside the children to give assistance when appropriate. Provide them with a 'master copy' showing the correct order for them to refer to while playing game 1. Colour the photocopiable sheet to provide more distinctive picture cards.

For older children

Provide an extra challenge for the children playing game 1 by providing them with a time-limit in which to complete the task. (A large egg-timer or alarm clock will enable them to observe 'time passing'.)

FROG JUMPS

Learning objective
To reinforce number recognition and to help develop counting-on skills.

Group size
Individuals or small groups.

What you need

Pictures of frogs, A5 stiff card, strong elastic bands, strong adhesive tape, PVA adhesive, scissors, card or fabric (approx. 1m × 1m), the song 'Five little speckled frogs'.

A5 stiff card folded in half

Setting up

Pop-up frog: Invite each child to make a pop-up frog. Fold in half a piece of card (A5 in size). The children should then draw, or cut out, a picture of a frog and stick it onto the card. Next, help them to tape an elastic band across the fold inside the card, making sure that the elastic band is held taut. To make the frog jump, just press down on the fold and let go!

inside of card (A5) showing elastic band taped at each end

Number pond: Draw the outline of a large pond onto a sheet of card (approx. 1m × 1m). Divide the 'pond' into four sections, and draw or stick a picture of a 'lily pad' in the centre (approx. 20cm × 20cm). Write a number in each of the four sections (the numbers will depend on the age and ability of the children).

Sing 'Five little speckled frogs' with the children. Place the number pond on a table.

How to play

The players take it in turns to place their pop-up frog onto the lily pad in the centre of the 'pond'. They then press down on their 'frog' to make it 'leap off' the lily pad and into the pond. If the frog lands in one of the four sections, they write down or recall their score. If the frog lands on a dividing line, or outside the pond, then they have another go. The winner is the player with the highest score.

When the children are familiar with this game, invite them to have two goes each and then to add their two scores together, the winner being the child with the highest total score.

Follow-up activities
- Find out more about frogs – what they like to eat, the different sizes and colours of frogs, the appearance of their feet, eyes, mouth and so on.
- Use clay, dough or Plasticine to create three-dimensional models of frogs, fish or other water creatures.
- If possible, visit a local pond to observe water creatures in their natural habitat.

Questions to ask

If you have one go, what is the highest score you can reach? What is the lowest score? If you have two goes and add the two scores together, what is the highest and lowest totals you can achieve?

card or fabric (approx size 1m)

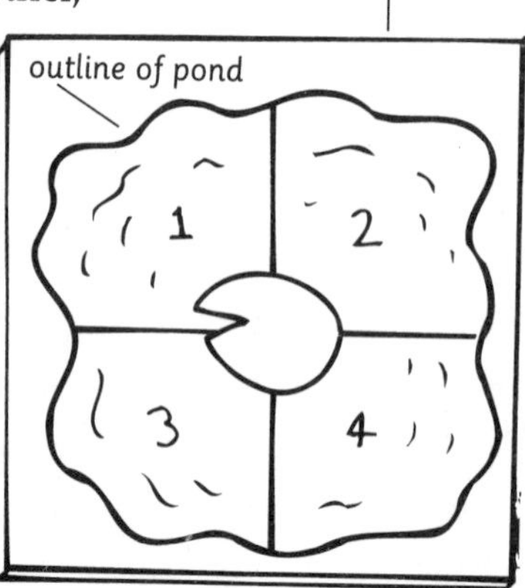

For younger children

Use dots or pictures (for example, little fish) in each of the four sections on the pond instead of numerals and encourage the children to count their score.

For older children

Use higher numbers, or give the children more goes. Ask them to record a series of scores onto paper, then invite them to use a calculator to work out the total score.

THIS LITTLE PIG WENT TO MARKET

Learning objective
To develop an awareness of handling money and giving change.

Group size
Two to four players.

What you need

Photocopiable page 62 (enlarged to A3 size, if possible), one counter per player, a dice (with dots, numerals or words one to six), 20p in change for each player (one 5p piece, five 2p pieces and five 1p pieces), a small box, 20p in change for the box (five 2p pieces and ten 1p pieces), felt-tipped pens or coloured pencils, plastic film, stiff card (the same size as the game).

Setting up

Colour a copy of the photocopiable game sheet using felt-tipped pens or coloured pencils (or invite the children to colour it in), then mount it onto card and cover it in plastic film. Lay the game sheet and the dice on the table. Provide each player with a counter and 20p in change. Place a small box (containing 20p in change) on the table in which to put the money for items bought and from which change may be taken.

How to play

Each player places their counter on any one of the 'stepping stones'. The first player throws the dice, and moves accordingly in any direction she chooses. If that player lands on a 'market stall' she may pretend to buy up to three items. The correct money must then be placed into the box. If the player does not have enough money to buy any items, the dice is passed to the next player.

This process is repeated, each player taking it in turns to throw the dice and move around the market place. The winner is the first player to spend exactly 20p.

Questions to ask

How many stepping stones are there to the next stall? How much money have you spent? How much money have you got left? Which costs more, three books or three flowers?

For younger children

Help the children to spend less money, say 10p, or provide all their change in one penny coins.

For older children

Provide the children with more money to spend, say 50p. Encourage one child to act as 'banker' to give change when required by the other players.

Follow-up activities
- Say the rhyme 'This little pig went to market'.
- Set up a role-play area to represent a market stall.
- Design a board game based on a favourite rhyme or story.

MARY'S GARDEN

Learning objective
To develop an awareness of mathematical terms such as 'most', 'least', 'how many', and to stimulate an interest in problem solving.

Group size
Individuals.

What you need

A copy of the rhyme 'Mary, Mary, quite contrary', A3 or A4 paper, felt-tipped pens or coloured pencils, black marker pen.

Setting up

Draw a grid as shown in the diagram onto a sheet of A3 or A4 paper using a black pen, and label it 'Mary's garden'. Photocopy one sheet for each child.

Say the rhyme 'Mary, Mary, quite contrary' with the children. Talk about her garden and what it might contain. Provide each child with a grid, and explain that it represents Mary's garden, with eight adjoining flower-beds. Invite the children to decorate Mary's garden by drawing one, two or three colourful flowers in each bed. (See diagram.)

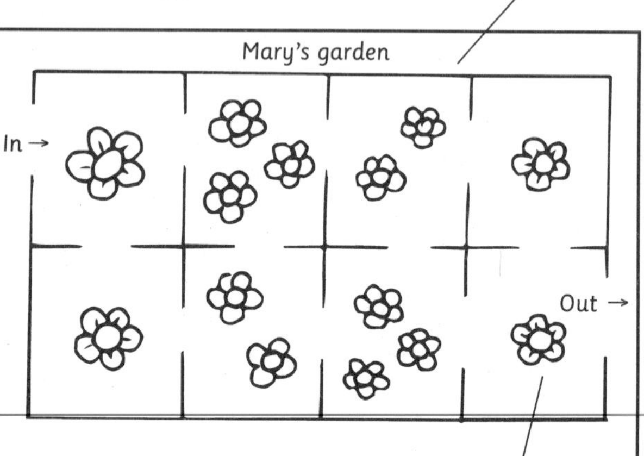

How to play

Mary walks through her garden picking flowers, but she never goes through a flower-bed twice. Ask the children to work out which way she should go to collect the most flowers. Which way should she go to collect the fewest flowers? When the children have solved the problem using their own grid, encourage them to use a friend's grid.

Questions to ask

How many flowers are there all together on your grid? In how many different ways can Mary walk through her garden?

For younger children

Let a small group of children help to decorate one garden. Encourage them to work together to solve the problems. Work closely with the children to explain the mathematical terms and phrases.

For older children

Invite them to decorate Mary's garden with 'shells' and 'flowers'. Encourage each child to think of a 'new' problem or question for their peers to solve – which way should Mary go to collect the most 'shells?'; which way should Mary go to collect more than two shells, and more than three flowers?

Follow-up activities

- Set up a role-play area based on a garden centre or flower shop.
- Make a selection of three-dimensional flowers using coloured tissue paper, fabric and so on.
- Construct a mini-garden in a shallow tray. Provide suitable materials such as soil, sand, moss, shiny paper, small mirrors, pebbles, twigs, small shells and lolly sticks.

INCY WINCY

Learning objective
To develop skills in counting on and counting back.

Group size
Two players.

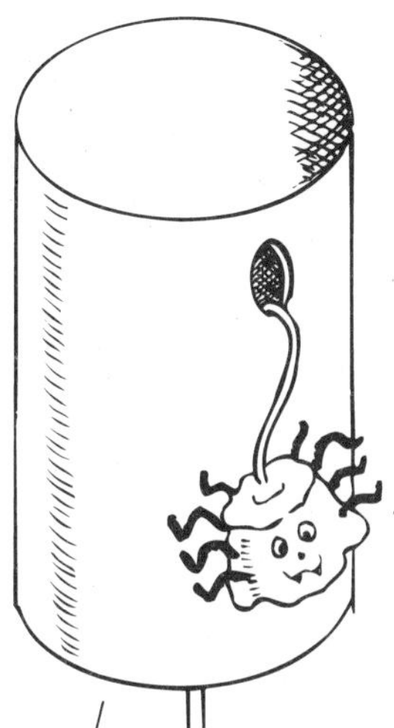

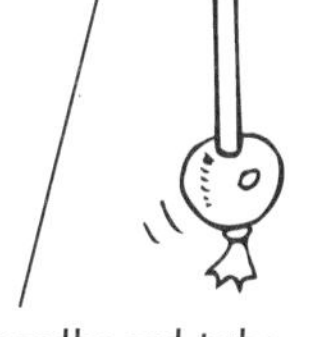

cardboard tube for drainpipe

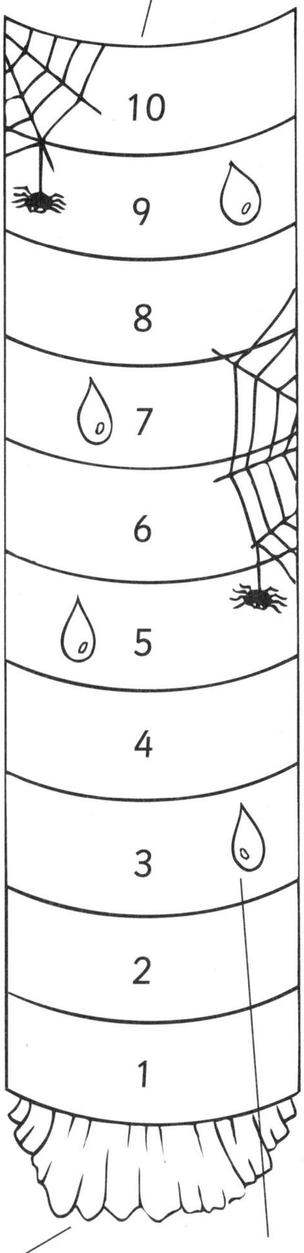

Follow-up activities
- Make a simple working model of 'Incy wincy'. Attach a length of wool to the 'spider counter' and thread the other end through a hole in the top of a cardboard tube. When the thread is pulled, 'Incy' climbs up the drainpipe. (See diagram above.)
- Go on a walk to observe spiders in their natural habitat.
- Read one of the popular Caribbean stories about 'Anansi', such as *The Illustrated Anansi* by Philip M Sherlock (Macmillan).

What you need
A strip of grey card (approx. 10cm × 40cm), a black marker pen, a blue marker pen, a cardboard egg box, pipe-cleaners, scissors, a dice (with dots, numerals or words one to six), light-blue tissue paper.

Setting up
To make the 'drainpipe' game board: Use the strip of grey card to represent a drainpipe. Divide it into ten spaces using a black marker pen. Write the numerals 1 to 10 in the spaces, with number 1 at the bottom and 10 at the top. Draw four blue 'raindrops' in any four spaces. If desired, decorate the drainpipe with some fine lines to represent cobwebs, and tape a little blue tissue paper to the bottom of the 'pipe' to represent water gushing out.
To make the 'spider' counters: Invite the children to make their own 'spider' to use as a counter during the game. Provide each child with a single 'eggcup' section from a cardboard egg box. Poke eight small holes in each 'eggcup' section for the children. Help them to draw 'Incy wincy's' face onto the cup and to poke four pipe-cleaners through the holes across the cup to give eight legs.

Say the rhyme 'Incy wincy spider' with the children. Place the drainpipe game board on the table within easy reach of both players.

drainpipe

10
9
8
7
6
5
4
3
2
1

tissue 'water'

shiny drop of water

How to play
The first player throws the dice and moves her 'spider counter' up the drainpipe accordingly. If that player lands on a 'raindrop', she should throw the dice again, and move down the drainpipe the correct number of spaces. The dice is then passed to the next player. The winner is the first player to reach the top of the drainpipe.

Questions to ask
How many raindrops can you see? If your spider is sitting on number 6 and has to move back three spaces, where will he land? If your spider is on space number 8, how many spaces does he need to climb to get to the top?

For younger children
If they land on a raindrop, ask them to move back one space. Use a dice with fewer numbers.

For older children
Double the length of the drainpipe, with numbers up to 20. Let the children use two dice to play the game.

egg-box section spider

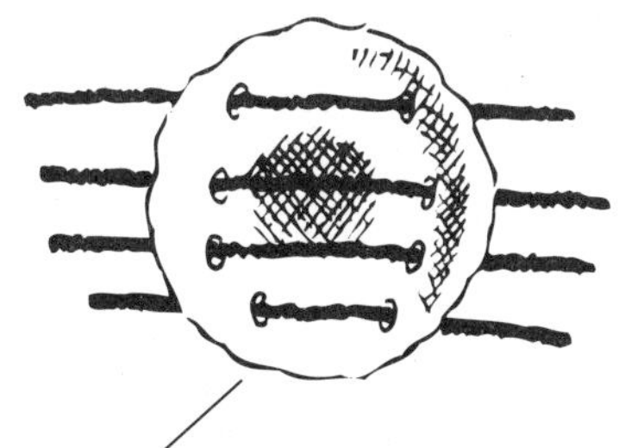

underside of spider showing four pipe-cleaners

FOUR BIG BUSES

Learning objective
To help develop number recognition, and to use mathematical language.

Group size
Two to six players.

What you need

The song 'The wheels on the bus'.
Buses: Four A4 sheets of paper or card (each a different colour).
Windows: 16 rectangles of white card (approx. 6cm × 8cm).
Wheels: Eight discs of black card (approx. diameter 7cm).
Two dice: One showing numbers 1 to 6, the second dice showing the four bus colours plus two white sides. (Note: The dice can be made from wooden bricks, with coloured or numbered labels attached to each side).

Setting up

Draw the outline of four rectangle windows (6cm × 8cm) onto each 'bus' and two round wheels (7cm in diameter). Number each shape 1 to 6 (see diagram). Invite the children to draw a picture of a face (or two) onto each of the 16 'windows' made from white card. (The faces can be drawn to represent best friends, parents or grandparents.)

Sing the song 'The wheels on the bus' with the children. Place the four coloured buses on the table. Ask the children to sit in a circle around the buses, then share out the eight black wheels and 16 picture windows among them.

How to play

The first child throws both dice. If, say, a 'yellow' side is shown on the first dice and a number 4 on the second, the player should place a window on the yellow bus in frame 4. If the number dice shows a 5 or 6, the child should match a wheel instead of a window to the appropriate coloured bus. If the colour dice shows white, the child is allowed to throw that dice again. The aim of the game is to complete all of the buses.

Questions to ask

When the game is finished ask the children to look carefully and decide on the answers to: how many faces can you see on the 'green' bus? How many wheels all together? How many faces all together? If the wheels are removed from the blue bus, how many are left?

For younger children

Play the game using two buses. Place dots on the dice, windows and wheels instead of figures.

For older children

Write addition or subtraction sums on the windows and wheels instead of numbers. Alternatively, introduce two dice showing the numbers 0 to 3 for addition. Or use two dice showing the numbers 1 to 6 and 0 to 5 for subtraction.

Follow-up activities

- Display a real wheel or tyre; observe and feel the patterns and textures of the tread.
- Make prints or rubbings of the tyre.
- Display a set of different types of wheels from bicycles, prams, toys and so on for comparison.

Opportunities for using games to develop the children's personal and social development are explored in this chapter. For example, children can improve their awareness of caring for their immediate environment in the activity 'Picking up litter', and caring for animals and developing a sense of right and wrong are highlighted in 'What should I do?' Multicultural issues are explored in 'Celebrations', 'Disguises' and 'Keeping clean'.

KEEPING CLEAN

Learning objective
To develop an understanding of the importance of personal hygiene.

Group size
Small group.

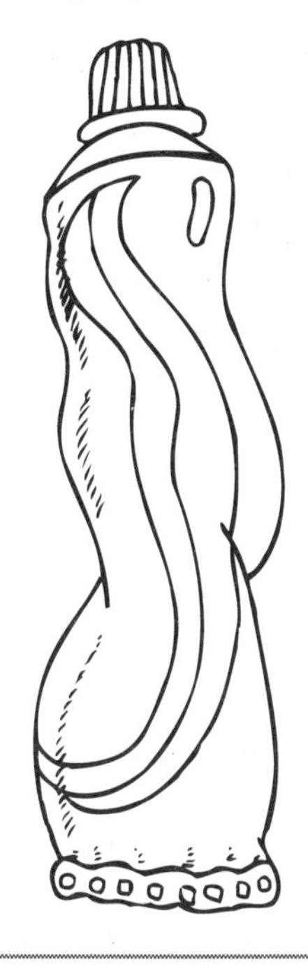

Follow-up activities
- Use a selection of appropriate liquids, soaps and powders to clean a teaset, some toys or doll's clothes.
- Find out how different animals keep clean.
- Find out about the different traditions and religious customs surrounding the theme of washing in other cultures.

What you need
A feely bag or box, a collection of familiar objects for keeping clean, such as a toothbrush, hairbrush, comb, back brush, flannel, sponge, tube of toothpaste (with an extra seal over the top to prevent accidental spillages), soap, small plastic bottle of shampoo (with an extra seal on the lid), hand towel.

Setting up
Display the collection of objects for the children to see and feel. Talk about what each object on display is used for, mentioning important routines such as washing your hands before eating and cleaning your teeth regularly. Children from different cultures may have some other traditional routines which they would like to share. When the children are familiar with the selection of objects, remove them from sight and hide one item in the feely bag.

How to play
The children take turns to feel inside the bag and to describe the object that has been hidden. Can their friends guess the object from the description given? When everybody has had a guess, the child who gave the description removes the item to see if she was correct.

Questions to ask
What do you use a toothbrush for? When do you use it? Why do you use it? What items could you use if you needed a bath? Is water important to help us keep clean? Why?

For younger children
Give verbal assistance to the children as they describe the objects inside the feely bag. For example, is it hard or soft? What shape is it? Is it smooth? Does it have bristles?

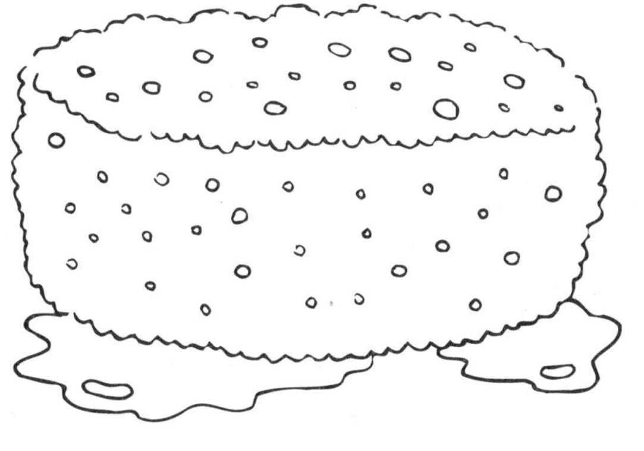

For older children
Encourage the children who are guessing the object to ask questions. Ask the child who is feeling the object to try to remember to answer the questions without actually naming the object.

THE JIGSAW BODY GAME

Learning objective
To become familiar with the names and positions of different parts of the body.

Group size
Two players or two teams.

What you need

Light-coloured card, black paper, felt-tipped pens or coloured pencils, scissors, magazines, PVA adhesive, a large doll (or puppet which is shaped like a person).

Setting up

Draw around and cut out the shape of a doll twice using two large sheets of card. Make two more identical shapes out of black paper to produce a 'shadow' image of each figure. Leave the 'shadow' images intact, but divide the original body shapes into various body parts to create two similar jigsaws.

Invite the children to draw, or cut out and paste, a selection of pictures to make small picture cards (approx. 15cm × 10cm). These should match the various body parts on the jigsaws.

Provide each player with a 'shadow' figure and the jigsaw pieces. Lay the picture cards face down.

How to play

The two players take turns to remove a card from the top of the pile. If the first player reveals, say, a foot, she should place one jigsaw foot onto her 'shadow'. The picture card is then returned to the bottom of the pile. This process is repeated by the second player.

If the body part shown on the picture card has already been placed onto the 'shadow', the player must return the card to the bottom of the pile without adding to her jigsaw. The winner is the first player to complete her jigsaw.

Questions to ask

Focus the children's attention to their own body and ask questions such as: what is this body part called? Where does it join? What is this joint called? How many of these body parts do we have?

For younger children

Limit the jigsaw pieces to about six: head, legs, arms, body. Talk about joints such as ankle, wrist, knee.

For older children

Talk about the name and position of body parts – neck, chest, hips, waist, shin and so on. Use written labels instead of pictures on the game cards.

Follow-up activities

- Read *Funnybones* by Janet and Allan Alhberg (Picture Puffin).
- When the game is no longer required, display the jigsaw as a mobile by attaching the pieces together with fine thread and hanging it in a breeze.
- Display the 'shadow' on the wall with the body parts written on white labels.

DISGUISES

Learning objective
To practise sharing and turn-taking, and to learn about being patient.

Group size
Three players.

What you need
Three items from three very different outfits (a policeman's outfit, for example, might include a hat, a tunic, a pair of gloves; a clown's outfit might include a colourful wig, a bright shirt, a red nose; a pirate's outfit might include a headscarf, an eye patch, a ragged T-shirt), a dice (showing the numbers 1 to 3 and three blank faces), a long mirror (optional).

Setting up
Label the items from each outfit with the numbers 1 to 3 – the headgear, such as the hat and wig, could be number 1, the facial disguises, such as the red nose and eye patch, could be number 2, the tunic, shirt and T-shirt could be number 3. Place the outfits on a low table, or on the floor, and ask the children to sit in front of them.

How to play
The first player throws the dice. If, say, a 2 is shown, she collects and wears any item labelled number 2 and passes the dice on to the next player. If a blank side is shown, the player misses a turn. Or if the player throws a 2 and has already collected an item labelled 2, she misses that turn. Play continues until all three players are 'in disguise'.

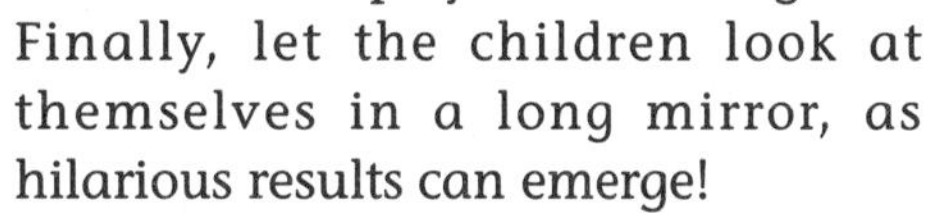

Finally, let the children look at themselves in a long mirror, as hilarious results can emerge!

The game can be played so that play ends when just one child is disguised in three items, that child being declared the winner of the game.

Questions to ask
Ask questions to stimulate an awareness of being patient. How will you decide who is going first, second and third? How should you react if someone chooses the item that you really wanted? If the dice keeps making you miss a turn, what should you do?

For younger children
Be available to help the children play fairly, take turns and be patient.

For older children
Provide an extra challenge by using higher numbers on the items and two dice for addition or subtraction.

Follow-up activities
- Provide a dressing-up area for role play.
- Can the children paint a picture showing themselves in disguise?
- Play the game using clothes, hats and jewellery to represent three outfits from three different countries. Talk about national costumes and why different cultures need different clothes (climate, religious customs and so on).

WHAT SHOULD I DO?

Learning objective
To develop care and concern for animals in trouble, to promote decision-making and to develop an awareness of our 'conscience'.

Group size
Two to four players.

What you need

A large sheet of paper or card, felt-tipped pens, a box, a selection of about six small toy animals, a counter for each child (use play people or small toy vehicles for counters), a dice (with dots, numerals or words one to six).

Setting up

Draw a pathway onto the large sheet of paper or card (use any design with a 'start' and 'finish' – write 'party' at the finish). Divide the pathway into 20 to 30 sections. Invite the children to turn the box into a 'vet's' (for example, by drawing windows and doors and adding a red cross sign).

Place the pathway on the table, positioning the vet's in the centre space or nearby. Place the six toy animals randomly on the pathway. (See diagram.) Explain to the children that their play figure or vehicle represents themselves walking, or being driven, to a party, and the six toys represent injured animals.

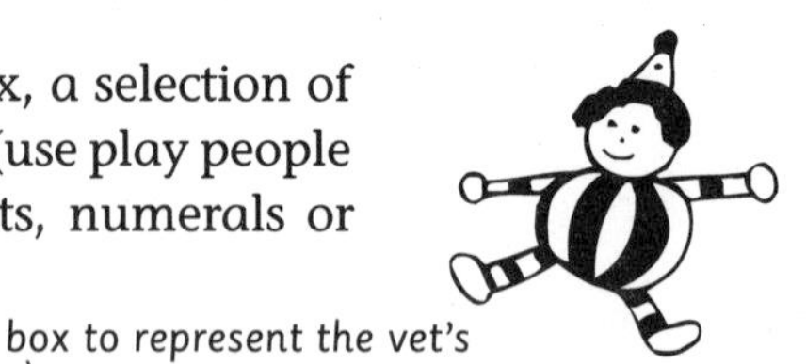

box to represent the vet's
toy animals placed along the route
start
party
vet's

How to play

The players place their play figure or vehicle on the 'start' square. The first player should throw the dice; if, say, a number 4 is shown, she should move forward four spaces. If the player lands on a space with an 'injured' animal, she must make a decision as to what to do, either leaving the injured animal on the path and moving on (that is, having another go) or taking the animal to the vet's and returning to the same space (that is, she does not have another go).

Play continues with each player taking it in turn to throw the dice. The winner is the first player to reach the party. However, is this person really the winner? Discuss this idea with the children.

Questions to ask

What do we think of someone who reaches the party first, but who decided not to help any injured animals on the way? What do we think of someone who reaches the party last, but who helped one or more animals on the way?

For younger children

Talk about what the children think is the 'right' thing to do.

For older children

Talk about our conscience. What is it? Have you got one? Is it important to have a conscience?

Follow-up activities

- Set up a vet's in the role-play area.
- Look after a pet that belongs to the group.
- Think about the welfare of wild animals by putting food out for the birds.

EENY, MEENY, MINY MO

Learning objective
To develop decision-making skills and to help develop co-operation while working in a group.

Group size
Small group.

What you need
Several sets of four or more toys (or pictures) – a set of animals, a set of cars, a set of trains, a set of small teddy bears and so on, a name card for each child, a shallow box for each set of toys.

Setting up
Put the sets of toys into separate boxes and place them on the table. Lay the name cards, face down, in a pile nearby.

Show the children the different sets of toys and talk about the meaning of the phrase 'a set of'. Encourage them to make 'a set of cars', for example, or 'a set of teddy bears'.

How to play
Arrange a set of toys in a row with an odd one out, for example a train among a set of animals. The players then say:

'Eeny, meeny, miny mo,
What does not belong in the row?'

Turn over the name card on the top of the pile and read out the name. This child then gets ready to remove the odd one out (some children may need adult assistance) while the rest of the group say:

'Eeny, meeny, miny mo,
Lucy takes it out of the row.'

Encourage the children to congratulate 'Lucy'. The name card is then replaced to the bottom of the pile, and the toys returned to their separate boxes. Repeat this process until everyone has had a turn.

Questions to ask
What is this a set of? Why is this toy the odd one out?

Follow-up activities
- Play the game using objects of different sizes, shapes, colours or weights.
- Talk about 'comparisons' – compare two dolls, two animals, two shoes and so on. Some pairs could be very similar, some pairs could be very different.
- During movement and mime, compare the movements of different creatures by, for example, hopping like a rabbit or wriggling like a worm.

For younger children
Encourage the children to co-operate by not calling out or pointing to the answer before 'Lucy' has had her go.

For older children
Encourage the children to take it in turn to put out the row of toys themselves. Challenge them further by mixing up the toys to create more obscure rows, for example a chicken among a row of four-legged animals, or a blue train among a row of white toys (this row might include a white car, a white horse, a white train and a white bear).

SPORTS DAY

Learning objective
To help build self-esteem and to develop the ability to cope appropriately with winning and losing.

Group size
Three players or three teams.

What you need

A selection of four wind-up toys, a wide table, card, masking tape, scissors, marker pen.

Setting up

To prevent wind-up toys from falling off the table, create a barrier by taping a fold of card to the edges of the table. Place a 'start' and 'finish' sign at each end of the table.

Explain to the children that the table represents a sports track and that today is a 'sports day'. Invite each player (or team) to select a wind-up toy. Explain that one toy will come first, and the others will come second and third, unless a tie occurs.

How to play

Begin each race with 'On your marks, get set, go!' Let the children have several turns, changing the wind-up toy each time. Encourage the children to congratulate each other, and to be pleased for the 'winner'. Help them to avoid feeling jealous or angry if they do not come first.

Questions to ask

How might someone feel if they come first? How might they feel if they come last? How can we help one another to be 'good winners' or 'good losers'?

For younger children

If the wind-up toys are awkward for smaller fingers use push-along toys. Help the children to work out how to push the toys to best effect – if they push too hard they might roll over, but if they are too gentle they may not reach the finishing line.

For older children

Encourage the children to work together to create new rules and instructions for the game. Invite them to keep a scoreboard and to make a good-humoured presentation to the overall winner, or to all those who took part.

Follow-up activities
- Hold a fun 'sports day' on the playing field.
- Paint a picture or create a collage entitled 'Sports day'.
- Create a circular obstacle course in the outside area for pedal cars, scooters and bikes.

CELEBRATIONS

Learning objective
To promote an awareness of celebrations from different cultures.

Group size
Three players.

What you need

A large tray, 30 brightly coloured card shapes (ten squares, ten triangles and ten diamonds, all the same size), a dice showing the three shapes (this can be made by placing six gummed paper shapes onto the sides of a wooden or plastic brick), examples of Eid cards decorated with Islamic patterns, if possible.

Setting up

Display the Eid cards that you have collected – this game is based on Islamic patterns, which are important during the festival of Eid. Look at the Eid cards with the children and talk about the patterns and shapes. Show them how the shapes tessellate.

How to play

Place all 30 shapes randomly on the tray. The three players then select a different shape each. The first player throws the dice; if the picture on the dice matches her shape, she may remove a matching shape from the tray to place next to her original shape. The dice is then passed on to the next player.

If the picture on the dice does not match the shape chosen originally by a player, the dice is passed on without the player collecting a shape from the tray. This process continues, the aim being to create a tessellating pattern using all ten shapes. The winner is the first player to achieve this.

Questions to ask

Which shapes fit together? If a circle was used, would it fit together with another circle? Does anyone know the special word that is used to mean 'fitting together'? It is 'tessellate'.

For younger children

Provide the children with a tessellating template to which they can match their shapes.

For older children

Play the game using more complicated interlocking shapes.

Follow-up activities

- Talk about the festival of Eid. If there are any Muslim children in the group, let them share their experiences of this special celebration.
- Find out about other festivals and celebrations from different cultures – the Chinese New Year, Carnival, Holi, Easter, Christmas, Passover and so on.
- Make shapes to create tessellating patterns.

PICKING UP LITTER

Learning objective
To inspire a sense of responsibility towards keeping our environment litter free, and to understand the effect of our own actions.

Group size
Small group.

What you need

A bag of 'clean' rubbish! – used items which are safe for the children to handle, such as a clean sweet wrapper, a clean empty plastic bottle, screwed-up paper, scrap of card, torn envelope, screwed-up paper bag, string, a straw, an empty drinks carton (with hole sealed with tape), a bottle lid (if not sharp), screwed-up paper tissue and so on. A playmat showing an outdoor scene (a farm, a town or a roadway, for example), some play people and toy animals and vehicles, a dice (with numerals 1 to 6), a rubbish bin or bag for each player.

Setting up

Lay the playmat on the table and ask the children to arrange the play people and other small world play items on the mat.

Talk about the scene the children have created. Then tip the bag of rubbish all over the mat (look at the surprised faces!). Talk about their scene now – has it been spoiled? Explain that they are going to play a game to clear it up.

How to play

Each child takes it in turns to throw the dice and to collect the appropriate number of items of rubbish to place in their bin. Play continues until the scene is tidy again. The winner is the child with the most items of rubbish.

Questions to ask

How does the scene look different with and without the rubbish? Would you drop rubbish? Where would you put a sweet paper? Why should we keep our environment tidy?

For younger children

Use dot dice instead of numbered dice to represent the number of items they can pick up.

For older children

Talk about the hazards of rubbish, for example wild animals may become trapped in bottles, cut on sharp edges of opened tins and tangled in plastic bags. Talk about the health hazard of dirty sweet wrappers on the floor or near farm animals.

Follow-up activities
- Arrange a 'keep tidy' campaign.
- Organise a collection point for recyclable materials – can ring-pulls and so on.
- Paint pictures of 'clean' streets, then collage rubbish all over them to show the effect of litter.

KNOWLEDGE AND UNDERSTANDING OF THE WORLD

The activities in this chapter can be used to inspire children with an interest and enthusiasm for finding out about the world in which they live. The third activity, for example, can help to initiate an awareness of minibeasts and their natural habitats. 'The honey bee game' helps children to understand the role and consequences of bees in our environment. Other games investigate themes such as capacity, colour and growth.

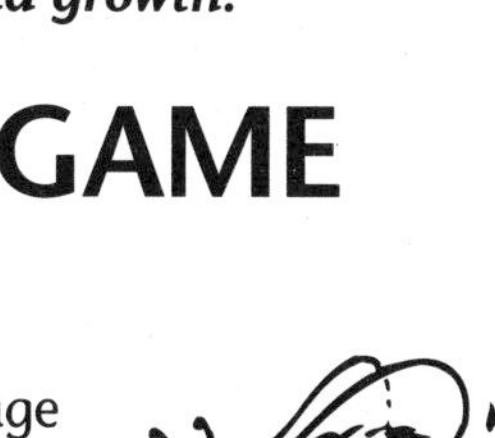

THE HONEY BEE GAME

Learning objective
To gain information about the honey bee and its role in the natural environment.

Group size
One to four players.

What you need

A copy of the photocopiable game sheet on page 63, felt-tipped pens or coloured pencils, scissors, a dice (with numerals 1 to 6), card, plastic film.

Setting up

Colour in a copy of the photocopiable game sheet (or invite a child to colour it in). Cut out the 'bee discs' and colour the background of each disc in a different colour. If desired, mount the photocopiable game sheet and discs onto card and cover them in plastic film.

Place the game sheet and dice on the table and provide each player with a bee disc to use as a counter. Explain that the game represents bees flying through the flowers to collect pollen to take to their hive.

How to play

The first player throws the dice and moves her 'bee' along the flowers accordingly. The dice is then passed to the next player. This process is repeated, each player taking it in turns. The winner is the first player to reach the hive.

Questions to ask

Ask questions that will evoke their interest, and use pictures and books to 'find out' the answers with the children: where does the pollen on a flower come from? How does a bee carry the pollen? Where does a bee put the pollen in the hive?

For younger children

Use dots on the dice or fewer numbers.

For older children

Ask them to make the game more challenging by writing short messages next to three or four of the flowers – 'No pollen, miss a turn', 'It's raining, move on four spaces' and so on.

Follow-up activities
- If possible, take the children outside to view bees 'at work'.
- Invite a bee-keeper to the group to talk about bees.
- Look at real honeycomb and taste some of the honey.
- Make a display of photographs, pictures and information books about bees.

ROLLING

Learning objective
To explore the 'rolling' properties of different shaped objects, and to develop an understanding of which shape rolls most successfully and why.

Group size
Game 1: *Individuals.*
Game 2: *Two or more players.*

What you need

Strips of card, a selection of box lids, strong glue or adhesive tape, scissors, a selection of small objects which roll and small objects which do not roll, a large tray.

Setting up

Fold several strips of card, cut into different lengths, and paste or tape the inner folded areas together (see diagram). Invite each child to make their own 'game box' by helping them to glue or tape some strips of folded card to the base of a box lid (see diagram).

Place the selection of objects which roll, and objects which do not roll, on a tray in the centre of the table. Invite the children to explore which of the objects roll most successfully across their game box. Then ask them to select one of these objects to play some simple games.

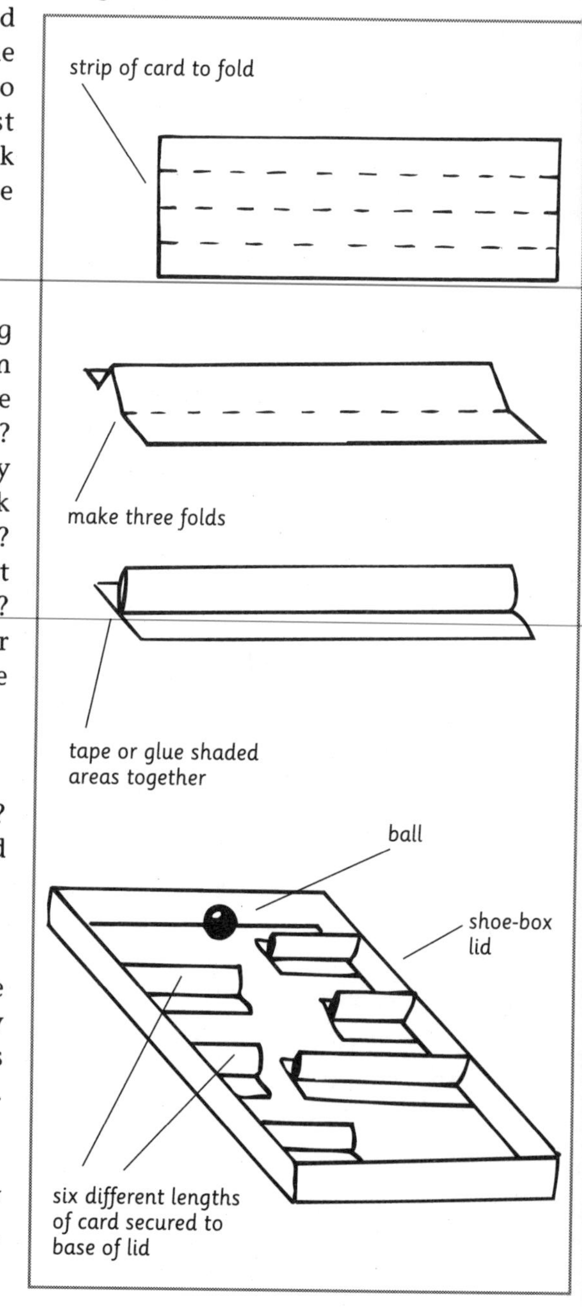

How to play

Game 1: Can the children, playing individually, roll their object from one end of their game box to the other before you count to, say, ten? Can they roll their object halfway across their game box and back again before you count to, say, five?

Game 2: Who can roll their object across their game box the fastest? Who can roll two objects across their game box and back again the fastest?

Questions to ask

Why does a sphere roll better than a cube? Can you think of your own games, rules and instructions?

For younger children

The children may need extra help with the construction stage, as it may be 'fiddly' for very small fingers. Let them make their own balls for their game, using Plasticine or play dough.

For older children

Talk about the names of the shapes that they explored, such as a sphere, cube, disc, cone, cuboid and cylinder.

Follow-up activities
- Decorate the game boxes using felt-tipped pens.
- Create a mobile from an assortment of different shaped, solid objects.
- Write the rules and instructions for other game ideas.

SPIDER'S WEB GAME

Learning objective
To stimulate an interest in learning about living things and their habitats.

Group size
One to three players.

What you need

12 card discs (approx. 15cm in diameter), 15 card discs (approx. 6cm in diameter), a dice (optional), black marker pen, a counter for each child.

Setting up

Draw a web onto each of the 12 card discs. On the reverse side of four of the webs draw some spiders (any number between 1 and 4). Then draw a large spider onto the 15 card discs.

Lay the 12 'webs' in a circle on the table. Place the 15 'spiders' randomly in the centre of the circle. Ask the children to sit around the table.

spider's web discs

spider discs

spider's web drawn onto each disc

draw 1-4 spiders on reverse of four card discs

draw one spider onto each of the smaller card discs

How to play

The first player places her counter on any 'web', then chooses a number between 1 and 6 (or throws a dice). The player should then move her counter accordingly. The web on which the child lands is picked up and turned over. If there are, say, two spiders on the reverse side, the child has to collect two spiders from the centre pile and match them to the spiders that she has turned over on the reverse of the web. If there are no spiders on the reverse side, the web is replaced and the dice passed on to the next player.

This process is repeated, each child taking a turn until all the spiders in the centre of the circle have been found a 'home'.

Questions to ask

Take the children outside to observe spiders and other minibeasts in their natural habitats: how many legs do spiders have? Where do spiders make their webs? Where do other minibeasts live?

For younger children

Sing 'Little Miss Muffet' or 'Incy wincy spider' to introduce the game.

For older children

Instead of drawing spiders on the reverse side of the webs, write the figures or words for numbers 1 to 4.

Follow-up activities
- Make close observational paintings or drawings of minibeasts in their natural habitats.
- Display a selection of relevant information and picture books about minibeasts.
- Create 'ink blob' spiders by dropping black ink onto slightly damp paper or fabric.

THE POSTMAN'S GAME

Learning objective
To acquire a sense of location and awareness of route maps.

Group size
Two to four players.

What you need

A sheet of white card, paper or fabric (approx. 60cm × 60cm), black marker pen, felt-tipped pens, four small boxes (base size approx. 15cm × 15cm), craft materials (coloured gummed paper, scissors, card, fabric and so on), small envelopes, four used stamps, a play figure for each child (to be used as a counter), a dice (with dots, numerals or words one to six).

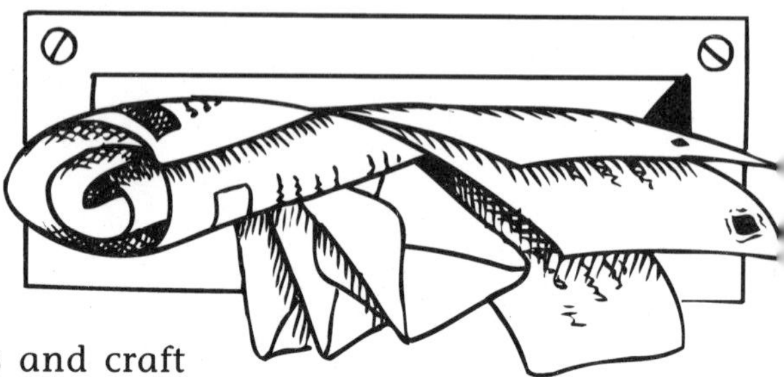

Setting up

Go on a local walk to observe postboxes, buildings with doors and letter-boxes, a post office and, if possible, a postman or postwoman delivering or collecting letters.

Provide the children with four boxes and craft materials to create buildings with doors and letter-boxes. Place the four 'buildings' on the paper and create a route map by drawing a road winding around the buildings. Divide the road into 20 to 30 spaces. Draw a path leading from each front door to the 'road'. Invite the children to use emergent writing to 'address' the envelopes, then add a stamp.

Give each player a play figure (as a counter) and two letters to deliver.

How to play

Each child chooses a place on the 'route map' to start. The first player throws the dice, and should then work out in which direction to move her play figure, the aim being to land next to a building to 'deliver' one of her letters. The players take turns and the winner is the first child to deliver both letters.

Questions to ask

How many spaces are there to the nearest house? In which direction is the nearest house?

For younger children

Let the children deliver just one letter instead of playing to 'win'.

For older children

Provide an extra challenge by writing a number on the buildings and envelopes. The players will then have to aim towards specific models before they can 'post' their letters.

Follow-up activities

- Send a letter or picture home, using the real address and a real stamp.
- Set up a 'post office' in the role-play area.
- Organise an emergent writing corner, with a selection of paper, cards, pencils, envelopes and stamps.

CHANGING COLOURS

Learning objective
To develop an awareness of how colours mix and change.

Group size
Two to four players.

What you need

A copy of photocopiable page 64 for each child, red, yellow and blue felt-tipped pens, small sheets of Cellophane (red, yellow, blue and clear – approx. 14cm × 12cm), a dice (showing the colours red, blue, yellow, orange, purple and green), a large tray, scissors, card.

Setting up

On each photocopiable sheet colour one of the pictures in red, the second picture in yellow, the third in blue and leave the fourth picture white. Then cut each sheet into the four separate pictures. (If desired, mount each picture on card.) Before the game is introduced let the children have 'free play' with the pictures and small rectangles of Cellophane to find out what happens when they place the coloured Cellophane over the coloured pictures. Talk about how the colours mix and change.

Provide each child with a complete set of the four pictures, coloured and cut out from a copy of the photocopiable sheet, to place, face up, on the table in front of them. Place all the Cellophane rectangles on a tray in the centre of the table.

How to play

The first player throws the dice; if, say, purple is shown, she should select one piece of Cellophane to place on top of her pictures. If she can make the required colour, in this case purple, then the Cellophane is left on the appropriate picture, and the dice passed to the next player. If she cannot make the required colour using this piece of Cellophane, then it is replaced on the tray and the dice passed on. This process is repeated, each player taking turns to throw the dice. The winner is the first player to cover all four pictures in Cellophane.

Questions to ask

What do the colours red and blue make? What does red and yellow make? What does yellow and blue make?

For younger children

Invite the children to play a very flexible version of the above game; they may need several attempts at matching different Cellophane colours to their pictures before the correct 'mix' is produced. Use only two players at a time, so that no one is kept waiting too long for their turn.

For older children

If the children are very familiar with colour mixing, challenge them to select and match the correct coloured Cellophane to the correct coloured picture, first time.

Follow-up activities

- Use primary coloured paints (red, yellow and blue) to mix secondary colours (green, orange and purple).
- Use black and white paint to create 'shades'.
- Select a painting by a famous artist and recreate it.
- Go for a walk outside to observe colours in nature.

FIVE LITTLE DUCKS

Learning objective
To explore and find out about the unique properties of magnets.

Group size
Individuals.

What you need

The song 'Five little ducks', materials to make a magnet game for each child: a very shallow box (such as the lid from a box or plastic tub), a strong magnet taped to a piece of dowelling (or thick card or a ruler), Plasticine, paper-clips, felt-tipped pens, coloured paper, tissue paper, PVA adhesive, egg-timer.

Setting up

Let the children make a Plasticine mother duck and five ducklings, then help them to press a paper-clip onto the base of each duck. Encourage them to decorate the inside of their shallow box to resemble a pond. Help them to make three or four 'water lilies' using scrunched-up tissue paper. These should then be stuck onto the 'pond'. The outside edges of the box can be decorated using green paper to resemble long grass or bushes. (See diagram.)

Sing 'Five little ducks' with the children. Then tell them to hold the magnet (attached to the dowelling) underneath the base of the box to move the ducks around the pond inside the box. Allow them time for free play to discover what types of manoeuvre they can make with the magnet and ducks.

Before the game starts, provide them with an egg-timer.

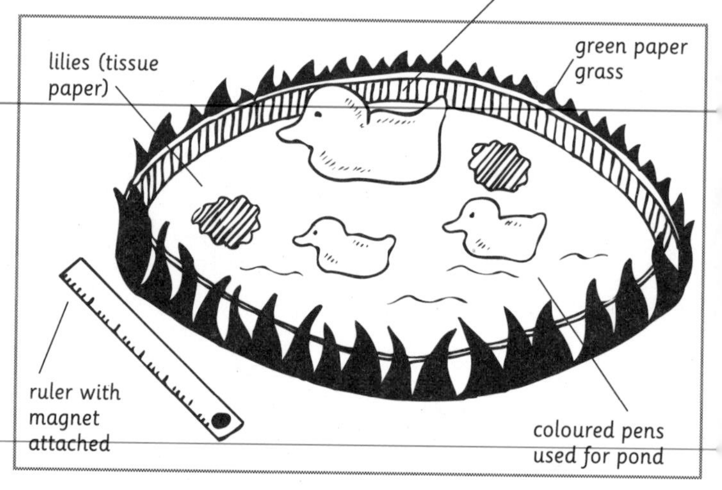

How to play

Set the children a few challenges. For example, before the time runs out can they move mother duck and all of her ducklings across the pond? Or can they make one of the ducklings swim three times around a lily?

Questions to ask

Which objects will the magnet stick to in the room? Which objects will not stick to the magnet?

For younger children

Before making the game, provide a selection of magnetic and non-metallic objects for the children to play with. Help them to sort the objects into the two groups.

For older children

Provide the children with a selection of objects. Encourage them to predict which might be magnetic and which might be non-magnetic. When they have found out, help them to record their results on paper.

Follow-up activities
- Construct other games using magnets, such as a fishing game.
- If possible, go outside to see ducks swimming in a local pond.
- Paint or draw a picture about the rhyme 'Five little ducks'.

CLEVER CROW

Learning objective
To initiate an awareness of capacity and how objects replace water space.

Group size
Two to four players.

What you need

Aesop's fable 'The Crow and the Pitcher' (alternatively, elaborate the story outline given below), a dice (with dots, numerals or words one to six), equipment for each child: plastic, transparent container (for example, a half-litre jug), an apron, a plastic shallow tray, a selection of solid wooden bricks or plastic blocks (all the same size), a small floating toy, kitchen roll.

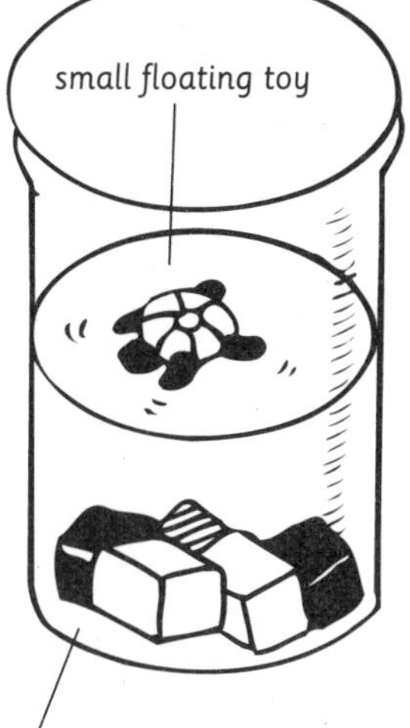

Setting up

Half fill the plastic containers with water and place them on the shallow trays lined with kitchen roll to soak up splashes. Drop a small floating toy into each container. Place a pile of bricks next to each tray and put a dice on the table.

Read the story of 'The Crow and the Pitcher' to the children. It tells the story of a crow who finds a pool to drink from, but the water is too low for his beak to reach. So he drops stones into the pool to raise the water level. Eventually he is able to reach the water for his drink.

Give each child an apron to wear to play the following game.

How to play

Each child sits in front of one of the containers of water. They will be able to see the toy halfway down the container, floating on the water. Explain that the aim of the game is to raise the water level to the top of the container and to retrieve the toy.

The first player throws the dice. If she throws a 4, for example, she should drop four 'bricks' into her container. The dice is then passed to the next child. Play continues, with each child taking it in turn to throw the dice, dropping the appropriate number of bricks in their container. (See diagram.)

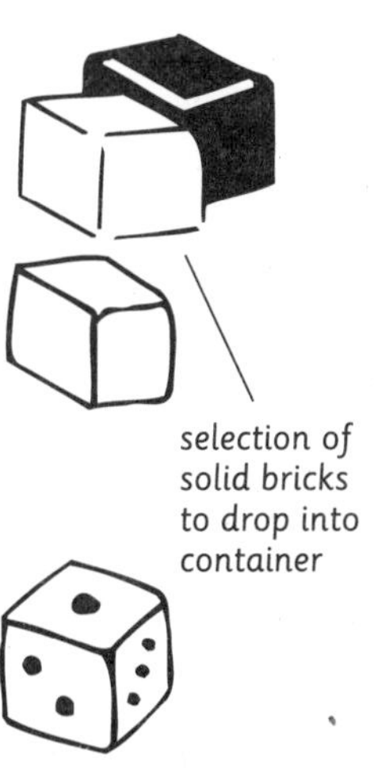

The winner is the first child who raises the water level to the top of her container and retrieves the toy.

Questions to ask

What will happen if you put too many bricks in the water container? Is there more water in the container when the level has been raised? How many bricks did it take to raise the toy to the top of the container? Will this number be the same if you use larger bricks or smaller bricks?

For younger children

Let the children play with the water containers using a selection of different sized bricks.

For older children

Encourage the children to predict how many large bricks or small bricks are needed to raise the water level to the top of their container.

Follow-up activities
- Experiment to find out what happens when containers of different shapes and sizes are used.
- Can they retell the fable in their own words?
- Paint a picture about the story.

A FOREST GREW AROUND

Learning objective
To become interested in plants and how they grow.

Group size
Any number of children.

What you need

A large cardboard box, scissors, felt-tipped pens, pots of soil (one per child), beans (one per child plus spares), a sunny window, water jug, the story of 'Sleeping Beauty'.

Setting up

Decorate a box to resemble Sleeping Beauty's castle (or invite the children to do this). Position the 'castle' on a table in front of a sunny window, and place all the pots of soil around it. Tie a length of string to the rim of each pot and secure the other end to a hoop hanging from the ceiling. (Alternatively, place the pots in a row along a window-sill with the string secured to the top of the window, and place a two-dimensional 'castle' behind the pots.) Tape four small minibeast drawings at regular intervals along one of the lengths of string. (See diagram.)

Read the story of 'Sleeping Beauty' to the children. Let them plant a bean in each pot around the castle so that they can grow their own 'forest'. (Keep a jug of water nearby and encourage the children to care for their plants.)

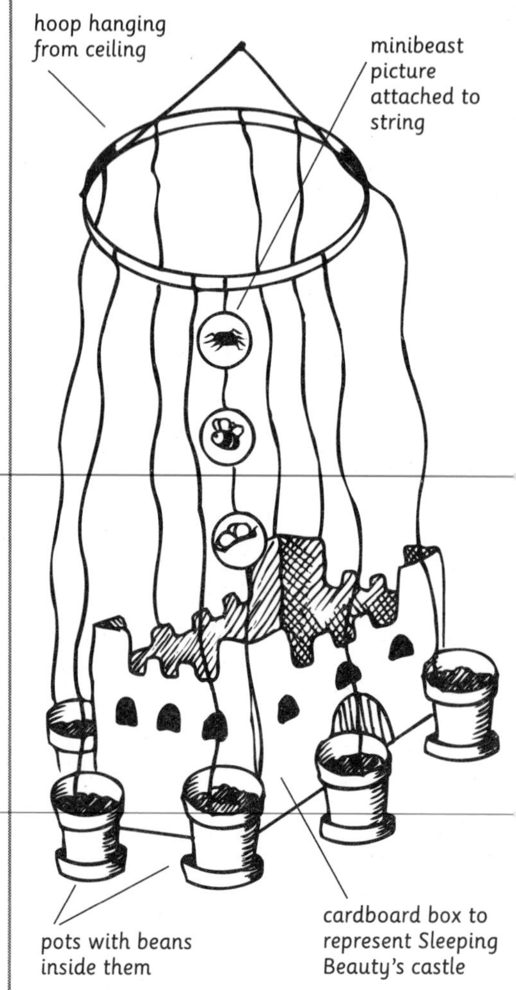

How to play

Each player guesses how high they think their plant will grow. The players then record their guess in words or pictures (with help from an adult, if necessary). They will then have to wait for their plant to grow to find out if their guess was correct. There is no need to establish a winner – the game can be played just for fun!

Questions to ask

What do plants need to keep them healthy? What will happen if you don't water your plants? What plants do you see in real forests?

For younger children

Examine the plants regularly with the children. Point out features such as the first shoot, the winding stem, the shape of the leaves and the pattern of the veins.

For older children

Encourage them to keep a regular pictorial or written record of their plants' progress. Place the minibeast pictures at known intervals – 25cm, 50cm, 75cm and 100cm – so that the children can monitor how tall their plant is in centimetres.

Follow-up activities
- Sing 'There was a princess long ago'.
- Plant seeds outside and care for them. Sunflower seeds and nasturtium seeds are easy to grow.
- Paint a picture of Sleeping Beauty's castle, 'hiding' it behind a collage of leaves and trees made out of different shades of green and brown fabric, tissue paper, paper, card, netting and so on.

PHYSICAL DEVELOPMENT

A range of ideas to develop fine motor skills, hand and eye co-ordination and manipulative skills are provided by the games in this chapter. Ideas for extending the games into the outdoor environment are given in the follow-up activities.

FEEL AND SEEK

Learning objective
To develop tactile awareness.

Group size
Small group.

What you need

A selection of everyday objects which are different in shape and texture (a woolly sock, a metal spoon, a plastic ball, a bath sponge, a cotton handkerchief, a piece of wood, a small brick and so on), a large cloth such as a tablecloth.

Setting up

Display the objects on a table, and let the children look at them and feel them. Then cover the objects with a large cloth so they cannot be seen.

How to play

The players take it in turns to feel under the cloth to identify one of the objects. Encourage them to begin by describing the object – its shape, texture, hardness, bendiness and so on – before identifying it. Let them retrieve the object from under the cloth to see if they were correct. If so, they should keep the object; if not, it should be put to one side. The winner is the child who identifies the most objects correctly.

Questions to ask

What do you think the object is made from? Does it have corners? Can it be squashed? Does it feel rough or smooth?

For younger children

Play for fun, rather than as a competitive game.

For older children

Introduce further challenges, such as can they identify the objects by feeling over the fabric? Can they identify the objects from a description given by another child in the group?

Follow-up activities

- Make 'sculptures' in three dimensions from clay.
- Provide very soft dough for pulling and stretching into different shapes.
- Talk about how important 'touch' is to blind people. If possible, obtain some Braille to see and feel.

A TANGLED WEB

Learning objective
To encourage the use of fine motor skills and to develop hand and eye co-ordination.

Group size
Individuals.

What you need

Hole punch, materials for each child: a sheet of card (approx. A5 size), colourful wool, felt-tipped pens or coloured pencils, adhesive tape, a dice (with numerals 1 to 6).

Setting up

Take each sheet of card and punch a ring of six holes around the edge.

Tell a short story about a mischievous kitten who jumps into its owner's knitting basket, pulls out all the wool and tangles it around the house. When its owner comes home, the mischievous kitten is hiding behind a tangled web of wool.

Provide each child with a sheet of card (on which you have punched six holes) and ask them to number the holes 1 to 6 on both sides, with adult assistance if necessary. (Note: the numbers on each side do not need to match – hole 1 on one side could be hole 4 on the other side, for example.) Encourage them to draw a picture of the mischievous kitten and the wool basket in the centre of the card on both sides. Attach a length of wool to one of the drawings of the wool basket with adhesive tape.

Before the game starts, give each child a dice to roll.

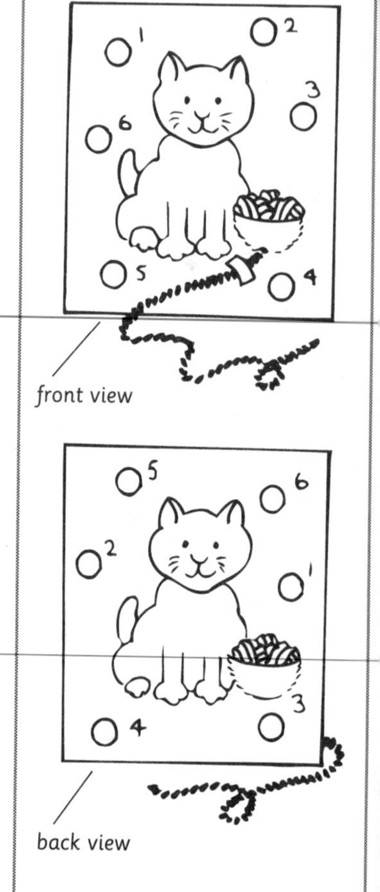

front view

back view

How to play

When the dice is rolled, if, say, 3 is shown, the player should thread the wool through hole number 3. She then throws the dice again; if, say, 1 is shown, she should thread the wool through hole number 1.

This process continues until the wool runs out. The mischievous kitten (on both sides of the card) should now be hiding behind a tangled web of wool. If desired, the children can unthread the wool and play again. (See diagram.)

Questions to ask

What happens if they throw the same number twice in succession? Does the tangled web look the same after each game? Does the tangled web look the same on each side of the card?

For younger children

The children may need help to work out the correct hole when threading the wool.

For older children

Provide 12 holes numbered 1 to 12, and two dice (both with numerals 1 to 6). Ask the children to throw both dice and add the score to find out in which hole to thread their wool.

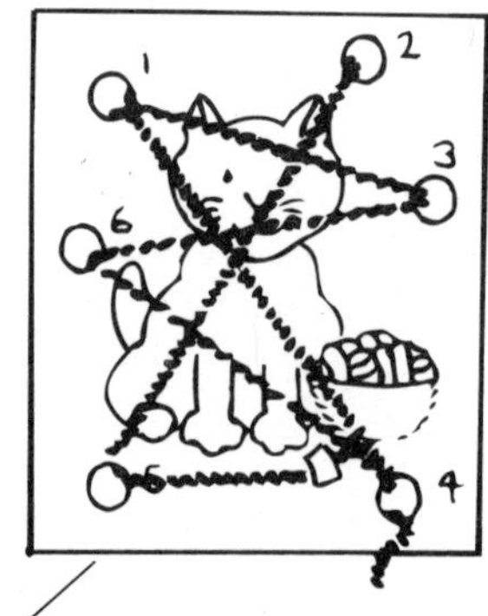

kitten behind a tangled web of wool

Follow-up activities

- Can the children retell the story of the mischievous kitten in their own words?
- Write the story or record it in at least three pictures, giving it a beginning, a middle and an end.
- Introduce finger knitting – challenge the children to knit something 10cm in length.

POT SHOT

Learning objective
To develop short distance throwing and aiming skills.

Group size
Games 1 and 2: *Individuals.*
Games 3 to 5: *Two or more players.*

What you need

A selection of small boxes and cylinders, thick card, PVA adhesive, gummed labels, felt-tipped pens or coloured pencils, paints or coloured gummed paper, counters (or similar shaped objects such as buttons or card discs).

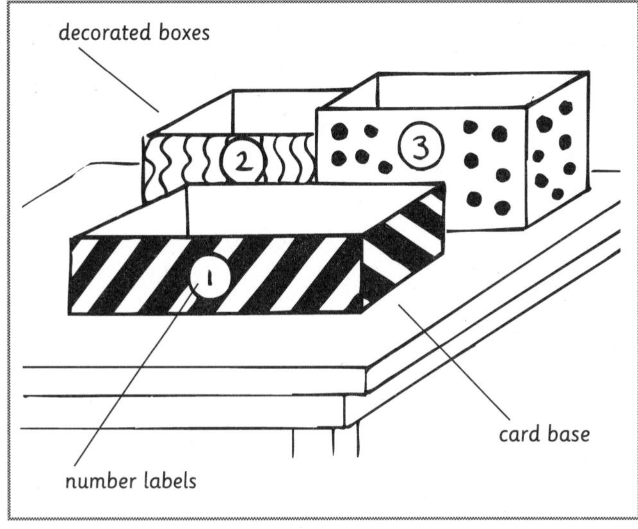

Setting up

Provide each child with two to four small boxes. Help them to stick the boxes onto a card base and to decorate them using paint or gummed paper. When dry, label each box with a number.

Ask the children to place one or more of the box arrangements in the centre of the table to play the following games.

How to play

Game 1: The player sees how many counters she can throw into the boxes in a set time.
Game 2: Using six counters, the player aims for the box with the highest number. She adds up her score, then plays again. Can she beat her first score?
Game 3: Provide each player with a set number of counters to throw. The winner is the player with the highest score.
Game 4: As for Game 3 but play three games. Add up the total score to find the winner.
Game 5: The players aim for a particular box (this could be the tallest box or the round box or the red box, for example) using a set number of counters. The winner is the player who has the most counters in the correct box.

Questions to ask

What happens if you throw your counter too hard, too high, too soft or too low? Do you throw better with your right hand or left hand? Which is the most difficult box to aim for? Which is the easiest box?

For younger children

Use the individual counters that have landed in each box to work out total scores instead of using number labels on the boxes.

For older children

Provide an assortment of objects to use as counters which are different shapes, sizes and weights. Let the children experiment to find out which objects are best for accurate throwing and aiming.

Follow-up activities
- Play throwing and catching games outside using an assortment of different sized balls, hoops or beanbags.
- Use fabric and lentils to make individual beanbags.
- Play games outside which involve aiming a ball, such as rounders, cricket, croquet and football.

JUMBLED JIGSAW

Learning objective
To develop co-ordination and manipulation skills.

Group size
Two to four players.

What you need

A copy of photocopiable page 64 for each child, felt-tipped pens or coloured pencils, scissors, PVA adhesive, thin card, a shallow box for each child (game 3 only).

Setting up

Mount each photocopied sheet onto thin card and cut it into the four separate pictures.

Provide each child with a set of the four pictures, copied and cut out from the photocopiable sheet, to colour in. Tell them to turn their first picture into a jigsaw made up of two separate pieces by drawing a line across it and carefully cutting along the line. (They may need adult help for this.) Help the children to use the same skills to turn their second, third and fourth pictures into jigsaws with three, four and five pieces respectively. Invite the children to use their jigsaws to play the following games.

How to play

Game 1: The players agree to jumble up a two-, three-, four- or five-piece jigsaw. They then jumble up the chosen jigsaw on the table in front of them. The first child to complete the jigsaw is the winner.
Game 2: As game 1, but the players jumble up two, three or four jigsaws.
Game 3: Each child jumbles up all four jigsaws in a box. The first player throws a dice. If, say, 3 is shown, that player may select any three jigsaw pieces from her box, and lay them on the table in front of her. The dice is then passed to the next player. This process continues. The winner is the first player to complete all four jigsaws.
Game 4: The players swap jigsaws and play the above games.

Questions to ask

How many jigsaw pieces are there all together? Which is the easiest jigsaw to put together? Which is the most difficult? Which has the largest pieces? Which has the smallest pieces?

For younger children

Let them divide all four jigsaws into two or three pieces only.

For older children

Invite the children to draw their own four pictures instead of using the photocopiable sheet. Encourage them to refine their cutting skills by creating intricately shaped pieces.

Follow-up activities
- Play with a selection of commercial jigsaws.
- Make a bag, box or folder for the storage of the jigsaws made in the activity.
- Provide a selection of different materials for the children to practise their cutting skills – silky fabric, tissue paper, card, Cellophane, felt and so on. Use the pieces to create an abstract collage.

FINGERLESS FUN

Learning objective
To explore gaining control of an object without using the fingers, and to develop an understanding of dexterity.

Group size
Two to four players.

What you need

For each child playing the game: a variety of five to ten different shaped and sized objects that are familiar (such as a piece of card, a sweet, a small brick, an eraser, a pencil, a ball, a ruler, a plastic cup), a tray, a shoebox, a pair of thick mittens.

Setting up

For each child, place the objects onto a tray on the table. Position the box next to the tray.

Invite each player to wear a pair of mittens to play the following games. (In both games, the objects must be picked up one at a time.)

How to play

Game 1: How many objects can the players place into their box from the tray in, say, one minute? Whoever places the most objects is the winner.

Game 2: Place the objects inside each box. Place the boxes on the floor, and the empty trays on the table. Which player can be the first child to replace all of her objects onto her tray?

Questions to ask

Why do you think it is so difficult with 'no fingers'? What everyday tasks would be very awkward if you were unable to use your fingers?

Follow-up activities

- Play clapping games and sing rhymes with finger actions.
- Create a display containing hand-shapes made by drawing around their hands onto coloured paper and cutting out the shapes; make a 'tree' using hands in shades of green and brown, a 'peacock' in shades of blue, or a white 'swan' with white hand-shapes for 'feathers'.
- Make finger puppets using paper or non-fraying fabric. Use for role play or during finger rhymes.

For younger children

Let the children have fun, at a non-competitive level, in trying to achieve the tasks set in each game.

For older children

Ask the children to look closely at their hands. Talk about how our hands help us to manipulate small and large objects with relative ease. Pay attention to features such as finger joints, the palm and the thumb. Talk about the dexterity of movement that is needed for different tasks such as picking up tiny objects, holding large objects and playing instruments.

UP, UP AND AWAY

Learning objective
To develop cutting skills and to create a 'new game'.

Group size
Two to four players.

What you need

A long sheet of blue card, six ovals of paper in six different colours (approx. A4 size), six large envelopes (unsealed), wool, card, comics and magazines, scissors, PVA adhesive, adhesive tape, two dice (one showing six colours to match the ovals, the other showing numerals 0 to 3).

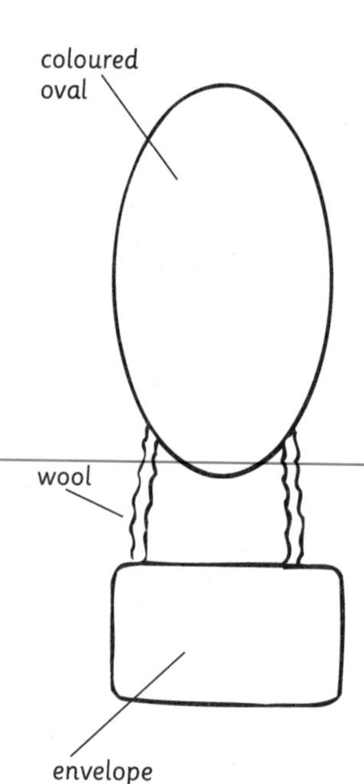

Setting up

Fix each coloured oval (representing a balloon) to an envelope (representing a basket) using two lengths of wool to create a 'hot-air balloon'. Secure all six hot-air balloons to the background sheet of blue card.

Ask the children to cut out at least 12 pictures of people or cartoon characters from comics and magazines to use as 'balloonists'. Help them to paste each picture onto card (approx. 10cm × 15cm). Use the balloons and balloonists to play the following games.

blue card to represent sky

clouds

coloured hot-air balloons

How to play

Game 1: Share the balloonists among the children. Explain that no more than two balloonists are allowed in each basket. The first player throws the coloured dice. If, say, red is shown, that player may place one balloonist into the basket belonging to the red balloon. The dice is then passed to the next player. If the dice shows the colour of a 'full' basket, the player misses that go. The winner is the first player to place all her balloonists into the baskets.

Game 2: Place all the balloonists in the baskets. The first player throws the number dice. If, say, the number 3 is shown, that player may remove any three balloonists. The dice is then passed to the next player. When all the baskets are empty, the winner is the player who has collected the most balloonists.

Questions to ask

During the cutting exercise ask: how can you cut around corners? How do you hold the paper while cutting? What is the most difficult part of cutting? How can we solve this problem?

For younger children

Make sure left- and right-handed scissors are available. Find out which type the children need. Show them how to use scissors safely.

For older children

Suggest that they cut out pictures and intricate shapes from wrapping paper to decorate the six balloons.

Follow-up activities
- Make up your own games together with accompanying rules and instructions.
- Use real balloons covered in papier mâché to make hot-air balloons in three dimensions and hang them from the ceiling to create interesting mobiles.
- Look at pictures and photographs of real hot-air balloons.

PICKING UP DIAMONDS

earning objective
o use tools in order to mprove fine motor kills.

roup size
ndividuals and small roup.

What you need

The story of 'Snow White and the Seven Dwarfs', 'diamonds' (shiny beads), a cardboard box, black paper, a variety of tools for picking up objects (tongs, tweezers, spatulas, spoons and so on), toy minibeasts.

Setting up

Cover a cardboard box in black paper to represent a dark hole. Put the 'diamonds' and 'minibeasts' in the cardboard box.

Read 'Snow White and the Seven Dwarfs' or read passages from the story about the dwarfs working in a diamond mine. Pose an imaginary problem for the children to solve. For example, one of the dwarfs accidentally dropped some diamonds down a hole full of minibeasts – how could they get the diamonds out without harming the little creatures?

How to play

Present the children with the box containing the diamonds and toy minibeasts and challenge them to take it in turns to find out which tools can be used to pick up the diamonds without scooping up the minibeasts at the same time.

Questions to ask

Which tool is best for picking up the diamonds? Which tools are not useful? Why?

For younger children

Let the children handle the 'minibeasts' to reassure them that they are only toys, as some children may be concerned about accidentally harming the 'creatures' with the tools.

For older children

Some children may enjoy making their own tools for the task. Provide a range of materials such as sticks, string, wool, adhesive tape, plastic spoons, card and dowelling.

Follow-up activities

- Paint a picture about the dwarfs looking down a dark hole for their 'diamonds'. Provide shiny paper for the 'diamonds'.
- Go outside on a minibeast hunt to observe the creatures in their natural environment.
- Read stories which contain minibeasts, such as *The Bad-tempered Ladybird*, *The Very Busy Spider* and *The Very Hungry Caterpillar*, all by Eric Carle (Hamish Hamilton).

TEN GREEN BOTTLES

Learning objective
To develop ball-rolling skills, focusing on hand and wrist movements.

Group size
Small group.

What you need

Ten small plastic bottles with a roll of green paper inside, sponge balls.

Setting up

Place a table against a wall. Stand the ten green bottles on the table in front of the wall.

Encourage the children to practise rolling the ball towards the bottles using a careful and controlled hand. Explain that they should then stand the bottles up again for the next person.

How to play

The players roll the ball across the table in an attempt to knock as many bottles over as possible. They are given a set number of goes before they pass the ball on to the next player. Play can be for fun, or a winner can be found by counting the total number of bottles knocked over.

Questions to ask

What happens if you roll the ball too fast or too slow? Is it easier to knock over bottles when they are in a row or in a group?

For younger children

Show the children how to use their wrist to control the ball, rather than their whole arm as used when throwing a ball.

For older children

Place numbers or colours on each bottle and ask the children to aim for particular bottles.

Follow-up activities
- Sing the song 'Ten green bottles'.
- Play rolling games outside using a variety of different sized balls and hoops.
- Create an obstacle course outside. Invite the children to take turns to roll a large PE hoop around the course.

A variety of different creative skills are introduced in this chapter through the construction of the games, for example toy making, painting and collage. Three-dimensional themes are explored in activities such as 'Mysterious monsters' and 'Mini obstacle course'. The importance of texture is highlighted in a game called 'Put the whiskers on', and the opportunity to design a game is provided in the activity 'The caterpillar game'.

THREE TOY BOXES

Learning objective
To experience designing and making a toy for use in a game and to encourage creative skills.

Group size
Two to six players.

What you need

For the game: Three shallow boxes (each a different colour), 18 labels (six of each colour to match the toy boxes and each label numbered, or with dots, 1 to 6), two dice (one dice with numerals 1 to 6, the other showing the three colours), a selection of commercial toys.
To make the toys: A selection of craft materials (boxes, fabric, card, pipe-cleaners, shiny paper, wool and so on), PVA adhesive, scissors.

Setting up

Encourage the children to use the craft materials to construct a toy of their own design – a puppet, an instrument, a robot and so on. These hand-made toys (plus some commercial toys to make up a total of 18) will be used in the game. First attach one label to each toy and place the toys in the appropriate coloured box. (See diagram.)

How to play

The first player throws both dice. If, for example, the colour blue is shown on the first dice and the number 5 on the second, that player should collect toy number five from the blue toy box. The players take it in turns to throw the dice and collect a toy. The winner is the child with the most toys.

Follow-up activities
- Invite parents or grandparents to the group to talk about toys from the past.
- If you have children from different cultures in your group, encourage them to bring in toys from other countries.
- Create an interactive display of toys for the children to sort, match, compare and make 'sets'.

Questions to ask

What sort of toy are you going to make? What materials will you need? How will you decorate it? Will you design it on paper first?

For younger children

To avoid disappointment, some children may need help with practical aspects such as cutting, gluing, sewing and so on. Otherwise, allow a high degree of independence as the children construct their toys.

For older children

Provide an extra challenge by encouraging the children to make a toy with wheels, a stuffed toy or a toy with moving parts.

THE CATERPILLAR GAME

Learning objective
To design and print an original number game.

Group size
Individuals or small group, then two players for the game.

What you need

The story *Creepy Crawly Caterpillar* by Margery Facklam (Little, Brown) or *The Very Hungry Caterpillar* by Eric Carle (Hamish Hamilton), sponges (cut into simple leaf shapes, approx. 10cm in length), paints, shallow tray, card (A3 or A4), scissors, dice (with dots, numerals or words one to six), felt tipped pens, gummed labels, small pieces of felt.

Setting up

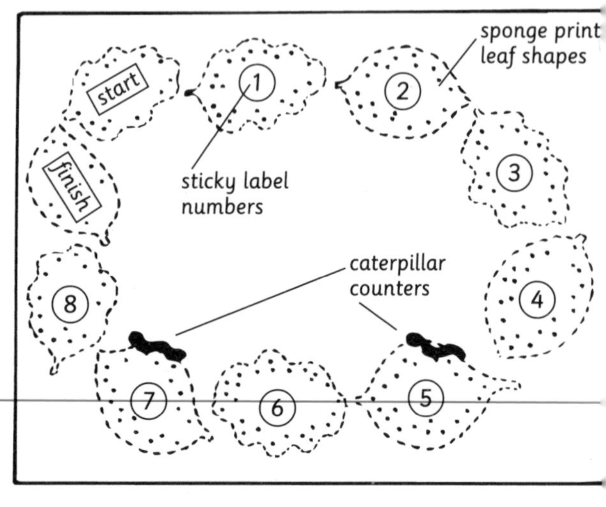

Help the children to cut out a simple caterpillar shape from felt (approx. 5cm in length). Put to one side for use as a 'counter' in the caterpillar game. Place a little green paint in the base of a tray for printing.

Read one of the 'Caterpillar' stories to the children. Then let them use the sponge leaves to print a simple design onto a sheet of card – for example a line, a circle, a figure of eight or a design based on the children's own ideas. When the prints are dry, help them to write 'start' on the first leaf and 'finish' on the last, using a felt-tipped pen on a gummed label. They can then write numbers onto their other leaves (the numbers should depend upon the age and ability of the children).

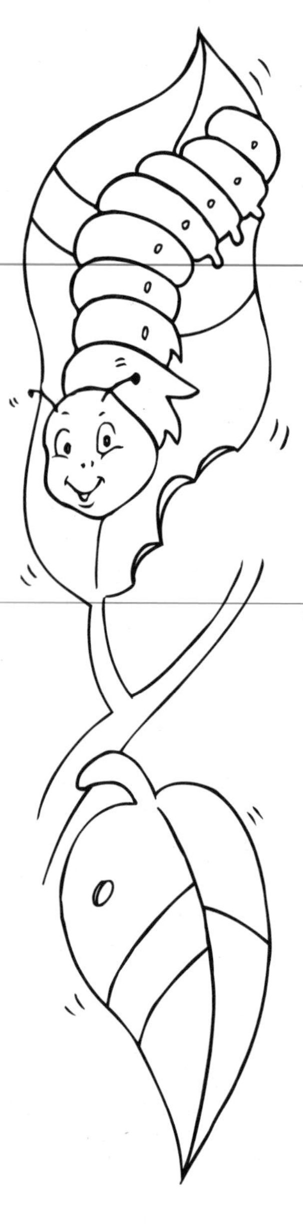

How to play

The players place their felt caterpillars on the leaf marked 'start'. They then take turns to throw the dice and move their caterpillar accordingly along the leaves. The winner is the first player to reach the leaf marked 'finish'.

Questions to ask

What are the rules for your game? Can you make the game easier or more complicated?

For younger children

Use the game to encourage simple counting-on or counting-back skills.

For older children

Ask the children to cut out their own leaf shapes from sponge. Provide two dice for addition and subtraction activities in the caterpillar game. For example, two dice showing dots or numerals 0 to 5 can be used for the addition of numbers from 0 to 10 when the children are moving their caterpillar counter. Alternatively, use a dice showing 0 to 5 and a second dice showing 5 to 10; the children can throw both dice before moving their caterpillar counter and subtract the smaller number from the larger number to give a value between 0 and 10.

Follow-up activities
- Collect leaves from outside to use for printing.
- Go on a 'nature walk', looking closely at the variety of different shaped leaves growing outside.
- Press some leaves, petals and flowers. Use them to make and decorate picture cards at a later date.

PICTURE STEPPING STONES

Learning objective
To inspire creative imagination and decision-making skills, and to make something useful.

Group size
Small group.

What you need

A selection of old cards, wrapping paper, comics and magazines with colourful pictures, scissors, PVA adhesive, card (approx. 60cm × 12cm), felt-tipped pens or coloured pencils, shape templates (approx. 5cm × 5cm), dice (with dots, numerals or words one to six), counters.

Setting up

Make an example 'Picture stepping stones' game board to show to the children before they make their own. Let them select any one of the shape templates (the type of shapes will depend upon the age and ability of the children). Ask them to place the shape over their choice of picture, draw around it and cut out the shape. They should repeat this process until they have approximately ten pictures. Then they can paste their pictures along their strip of card to create their game board. Provide the children with counters and dice.

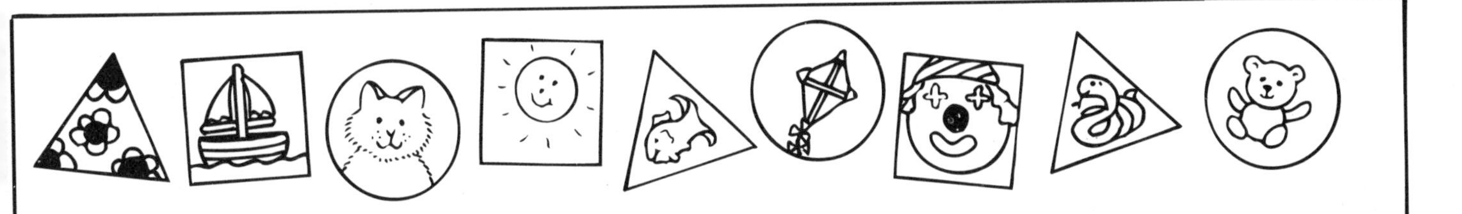

How to play

The players use their game board, counters and dice to play simple games with each other. For example, each player places a counter on the first stepping stone. They then take it in turns to throw the dice and move accordingly along the stepping stones. The winner is the first player to reach the last stepping stone. Let the children make up their own game if they wish, or their own rules such as 'Throw a six to start'.

Questions to ask

Can you describe the pictures on your game? Why did you choose those pictures? Which shapes did you use?

For younger children

Some children might find it easier to cut out an 'irregular' shape around their chosen pictures instead of using templates.

For older children

The children may wish to write 'start' and 'finish' on the first and last pictures, or to write numbers along the pictures. Encourage them to add messages along their game board, such as 'Have another go', 'Miss a turn', 'Go back to start'. Invite them to make their own number spinner, or dice using gummed labels on a wooden brick, and counters incorporating their own ideas.

Follow-up activities

- Decorate a box or bag in which each game can be stored.
- Play a selection of traditional, commercial games such as Ludo, Dominoes, Happy Families, Snap and so on.
- Talk about the names of the different shape templates. Compare the number of sides and corners of each shape.

MINI OBSTACLE COURSE

Learning objective
To construct a game in three dimensions of their own design.

Group size
Individuals or small group.

What you need
A range of very shallow boxes or box lids (approx. 20cm × 20cm), a selection of small three-dimensional objects (plastic bottle-tops, matchboxes, wooden bricks and so on), strong adhesive, small balls (such as ping-pong balls), straws, Blu-Tack, paints (or quick-drying spray paint for adult use only), small self-adhesive shapes or stickers.

Setting up
Stimulate the children's interest by making an example game for them to play with, then provide each child with a shallow box or lid, a selection of small three-dimensional objects and a small ball. Show them how to temporarily position their objects on the lid using Blu-Tack and then test their game by making sure the ball can move freely around the obstacles. If the ball gets stuck, they can reposition the objects.

When they are happy with the design, help them to remove the objects one at a time to fix in place with adhesive. After allowing these to dry, the games can be painted (or sprayed by an adult using quick-drying paint) and then decorated using small, self-adhesive shapes or stickers.

How to play
The players roll their ball or use a straw to blow their ball around their mini-obstacle course. Invite them to provide their own challenges or use the questions below to stimulate game ideas.

Questions to ask
Can you roll or blow the ball around every object without letting the ball stop? How quickly can you make your ball go around every obstacle? Which is faster – rolling or blowing the ball?

For younger children
Let the children work in pairs to create a shared game.

For older children
Suggest that they include number stickers on the base of their game so that they can score points as their ball rolls over the numbers.

Follow-up activities
- Construct three-dimensional models and shapes out of clay, play dough and Plasticine.
- Provide junk materials such as large boxes, tubes and tubs to make large structures and models.
- Create walk-in three-dimensional structures using sheets and other 'den making' equipment.

THE MUSIC GAME

Learning objective
To become interested in music and playing instruments, and to develop confidence and creative expression.

Group size
Small group.

What you need

A percussion instrument for each child, card (approx. A5 size), pencils, felt-tipped pens, an old nursery rhyme book (optional).

Setting up

Write a name card for each child, draw four 'smiley face' cards, make six nursery rhyme picture cards (these can be hand drawn, traced or cut out of an old nursery rhyme book) and draw a music note on three cards.

Provide each child with an instrument. Place the name cards and smiley face cards in one pile, face down, on the table. Make a second pile using the nursery rhyme cards and music note cards.

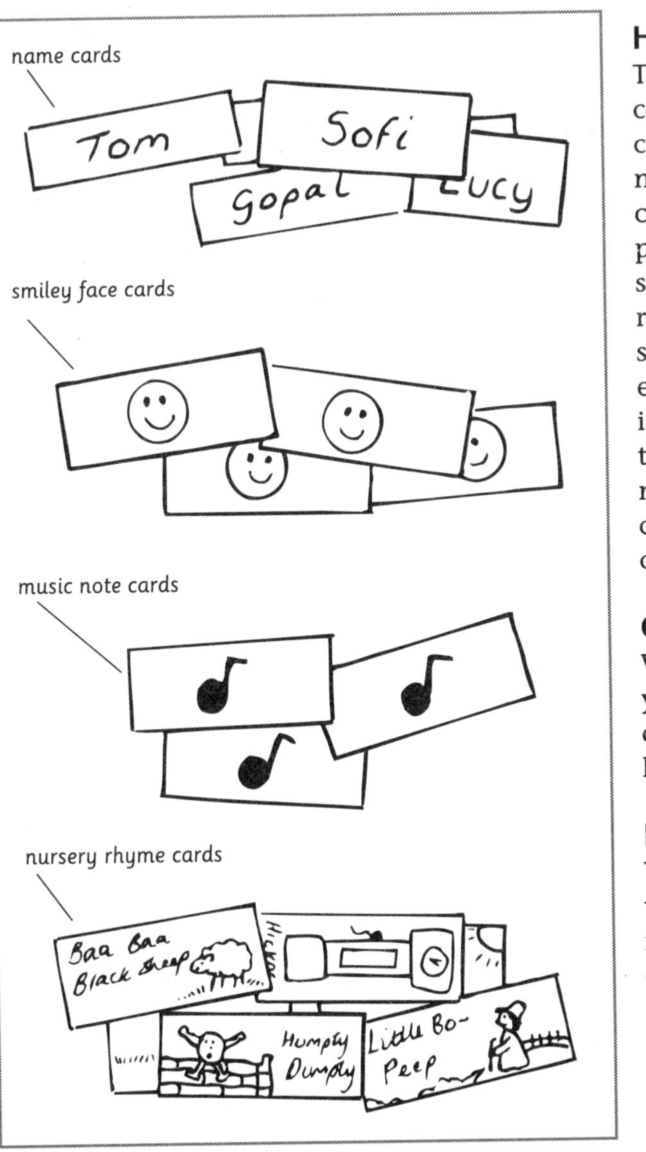

How to play

The first player turns over the top card from both piles of cards. If the card from the first pile shows a name, for example Tom, and the card from the second pile shows a picture of, say, 'Jack and Jill', then Tom should use his instrument to play the rhythm of the Jack and Jill tune. If a smiley face card is shown, then everyone in the group plays their instruments. If a music note is shown, the named child or whole group can make up a tune of their own. Play continues until everyone has had one or two turns to play on their own.

Questions to ask

What is your favourite tune? What is your favourite instrument? What type of music do you enjoy listening to at home?

For younger children

You may need to read their name for them and play an instrument alongside individuals to help build their confidence.

For older children

Let them prepare the name and picture cards for the game.

Follow-up activities

- Provide a variety of materials for the children to make their own percussion instruments.
- Listen to a variety of music – classical, pop, big band, choral – and talk about it, encouraging the children to give personal opinions.
- Provide a cassette recorder so that the children can record themselves playing different instruments.

PUT THE WHISKERS ON

Learning objective
To co-operate together to create a game to share, and to increase awareness of different materials and textures.

Group size
Small group.

What you need
A large sheet of paper or card (approx. A1 size), fabric swatches (including different textures such as felt, fur and silky fabric), felt-tipped pens or coloured pencils, paper straws, two large buttons, card, scissors, PVA adhesive, marker pen, a blindfold (optional).

Setting up
Draw the outline of a mouse, keeping it very simple. Invite the children to decorate the mouse using a variety of materials that have different textures, perhaps giving it a silky tail, felt or fur for its ears and buttons for its eyes and nose. Let them include straw 'whiskers' on only one side of the mouse; leave the other side whiskerless! Help the children to paste straw whiskers onto a separate section of card to represent the 'missing' whiskers. Lay the decorated mouse on a table.

separate section of card with straw whiskers

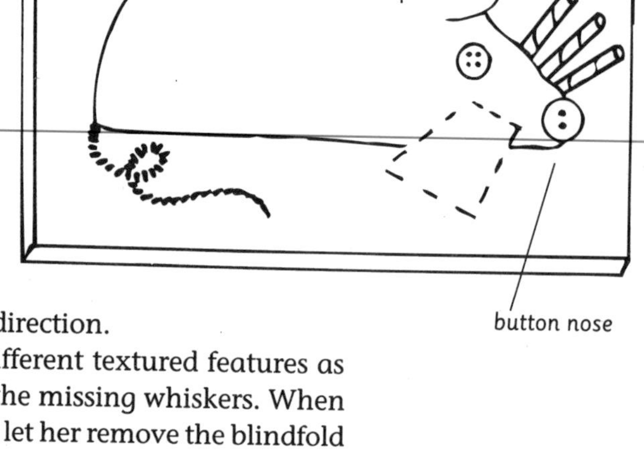

How to play
Place a blindfold on the first player (or ask the child to close her eyes) and ask the rest of the children to twist the mouse around so that it is facing in a different direction.

The first player should then use the different textured features as 'feely' clues for assessing where to place the missing whiskers. When she has placed the whiskers on the mouse, let her remove the blindfold to see the result! Then the other players take their turn.

Questions to ask
What can you feel? What part of the mouse do you think it is? Where do you think the whiskers should go?

For younger children
Work alongside the children and talk about the feel of the different materials. Ask them to describe the textures. Emphasise that it is a game for fun, and that it does not matter if they place the whiskers in the 'wrong' place.

For older children
Let them draw the outline of the mouse and select their own choice of textured materials.

Follow-up activities
- Make cat and mouse face masks for role play and activities involving drama.
- Real mice are small and delicate, but imaginary 'monster mice' can be any shape, size or colour. Provide a wide selection of craft materials to create three-dimensional models.
- If possible, show a pet mouse to the children.

OFF TO SEA

Learning objective
To design and make a soft toy and other components for a new game.

Group size
Small group, then two players for the game.

What you need

The rhyme 'The Owl and the Pussy-cat' by Edward Lear, non-fraying fabric pieces (each cut into a rectangle approx. 25cm × 35 cm), sewing thread, needles, soft toy stuffing, small pieces of coloured felt, scissors, paper (approx. 25cm × 35cm), pencils, adhesive, a sheet of plain fabric or card or paper (approx. 1m × 1m), a marker pen, small cereal boxes (available in variety packs of eight), green paint, a dice (with dots, numerals or words one to six).

Setting up

Draw the outline of an island in the centre of the large sheet of fabric. Draw a wavy 'track' spiralling around the island to represent the sea. Divide this sea track into 20 to 30 spaces. Put to one side for later use. Make sure that each space is large enough for a small cereal box (approx. 10cm × 7cm) to be placed in it.

Read the rhyme 'The Owl and the Pussy-cat' to the children. Let them make an owl or a pussy-cat 'pattern' by drawing an oval shape onto paper and cutting it out (approx. 10cm in height). Help them to pin their paper pattern onto two rectangles of non-fraying fabric and to cut out two fabric ovals, then to sew their fabric shapes together, leaving a gap for stuffing. When the stuffing has been placed in their shape, help them to sew up the gap. Let them cut out shapes from felt to represent the features of an owl or a pussy-cat. Then help them to cover half a cereal box in green paint (this represents the 'pea-green boat'). Explain that their 'owl or 'pussy-cat' can now sit in their 'pea-green boat' for use as a large counter during the game.

child-made soft toys

How to play

Two children play the game, one with an 'owl' the other with a 'pussy-cat'. The first player throws the dice and moves her owl accordingly around the sea track. The dice is then passed to the next player. This process is repeated. The winner is the first player to reach the island.

Questions to ask

What else did the Owl and the Pussy-cat have in their pea-green boat? How could you make the game more complicated?

For younger children

Help them to glue their soft toy together instead of sewing it.

For older children

Let them draw their own island and sea track onto the large sheet of fabric. Help them to include simple instructions on some of the spaces, for example 'The boat makes good progress, move on three spaces'.

Follow-up activities
- Use the stuffed toys for creative play.
- Turn the role-play area into a 'pea-green boat' by assembling some green card around a group of chairs. Take turns to play inside the boat by pretending to be the Owl and the Pussy-cat rowing out to sea.

MYSTERIOUS MONSTERS

Learning objective
To create a model in three dimensions and to develop creative imagination.

Group size
Small group.

What you need

Plasticine (rolled into small balls about the size of a ping-pong ball), small containers, six varieties of small decorative objects which can be stuck into Plasticine (such as modelling matchsticks, buttons, beads, small lengths of string and wool, shapes cut out from thick card and short lengths of old chain), card discs, felt-tipped pens, gummed labels, small bag, a modelling board or mat for each child.

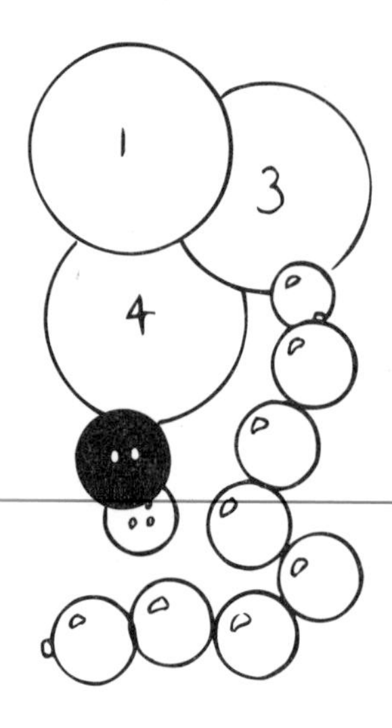

Setting up

Divide the small decorative objects into six groups and place them in separate containers labelled 1 to 6. Write the numbers 1 to 6 onto six card discs and place them in a small bag. Provide each child with three balls of Plasticine and a modelling board or mat.

Explain to the children that they are going to play a game to turn their three balls of Plasticine into a 'mysterious monster'.

How to play

All the players begin the game by moulding their balls of Plasticine into any shape they choose for a monster's head and body. The first player then removes one disc from the bag. If the number on the disc is, say, 2, that player may select one item from container 2.

This item should be used on the Plasticine body to help create their mysterious monster. The disc is then returned to the bag for the next player. This process is repeated, with the players taking it in turns to select a disc and the corresponding object.

There is no time-limit to the game; this will depend on the interest, age and ability of the players. However, about six goes each usually produces interesting results. After, say, six goes, invite the children to show everyone their 'mysterious monster'. Put them on display for a while before dismantling them and returning the decorative objects to their six containers, ready for another game.

Questions to ask

What is your monster called? Can you describe your monster? Is it fierce or friendly?

Follow-up activities
- Draw or paint a picture of your 'mysterious monster'.
- Write a story about monsters who have different characteristics, perhaps the 'friendly monster' or the 'fierce monster'.
- Read *Not now, Bernard* by David McKee (Red Fox).

For younger children

Use coloured discs with corresponding colours on the containers instead of numbers.

For older children

Write a message on each disc to replace the numbers – 'Pick up four matchsticks', 'Choose five strands of wool', 'Find two triangle shapes' and so on.

PHOTOCOPIABLES

Name ______________________

Name ______________________________

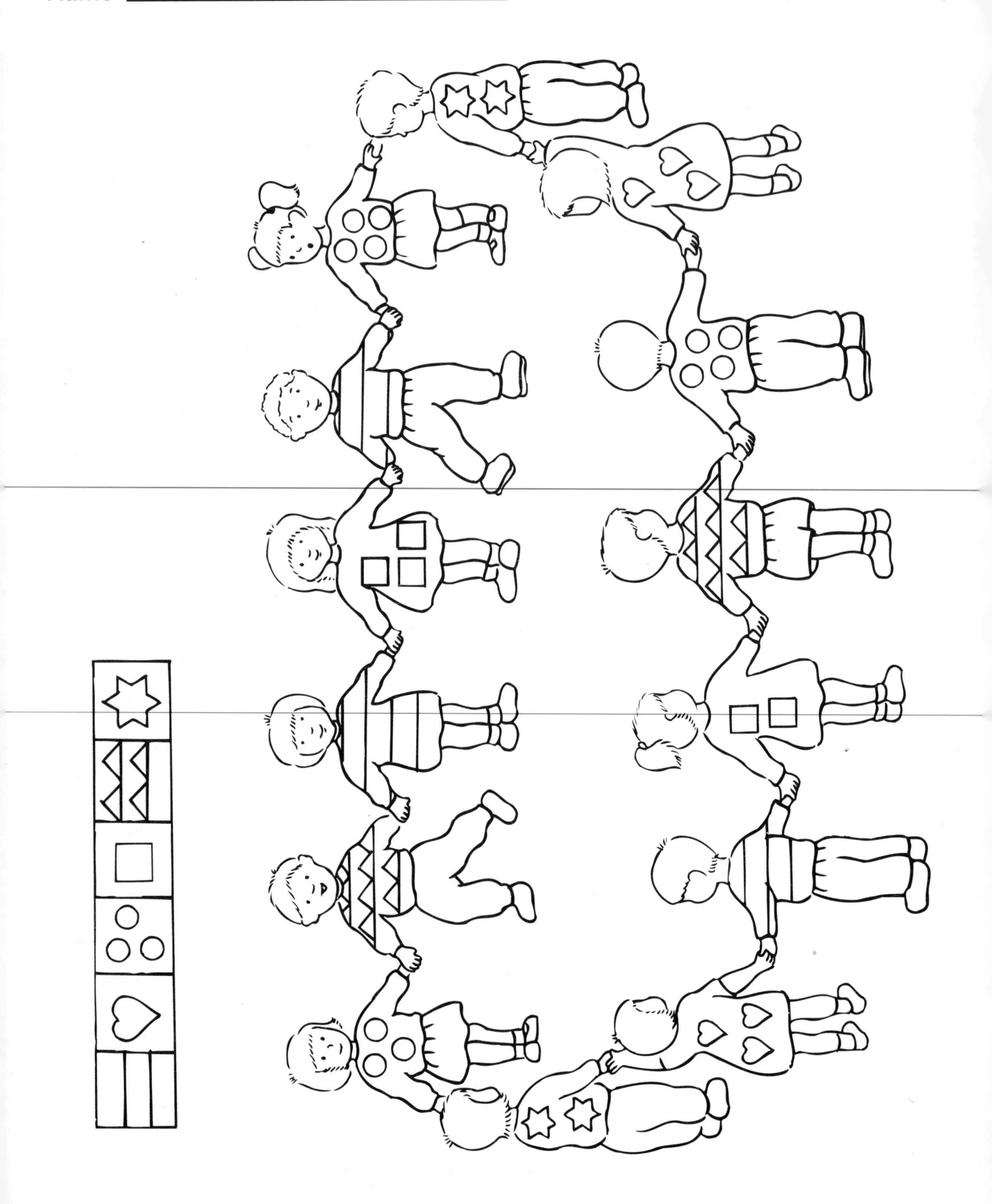

Name ______________________________

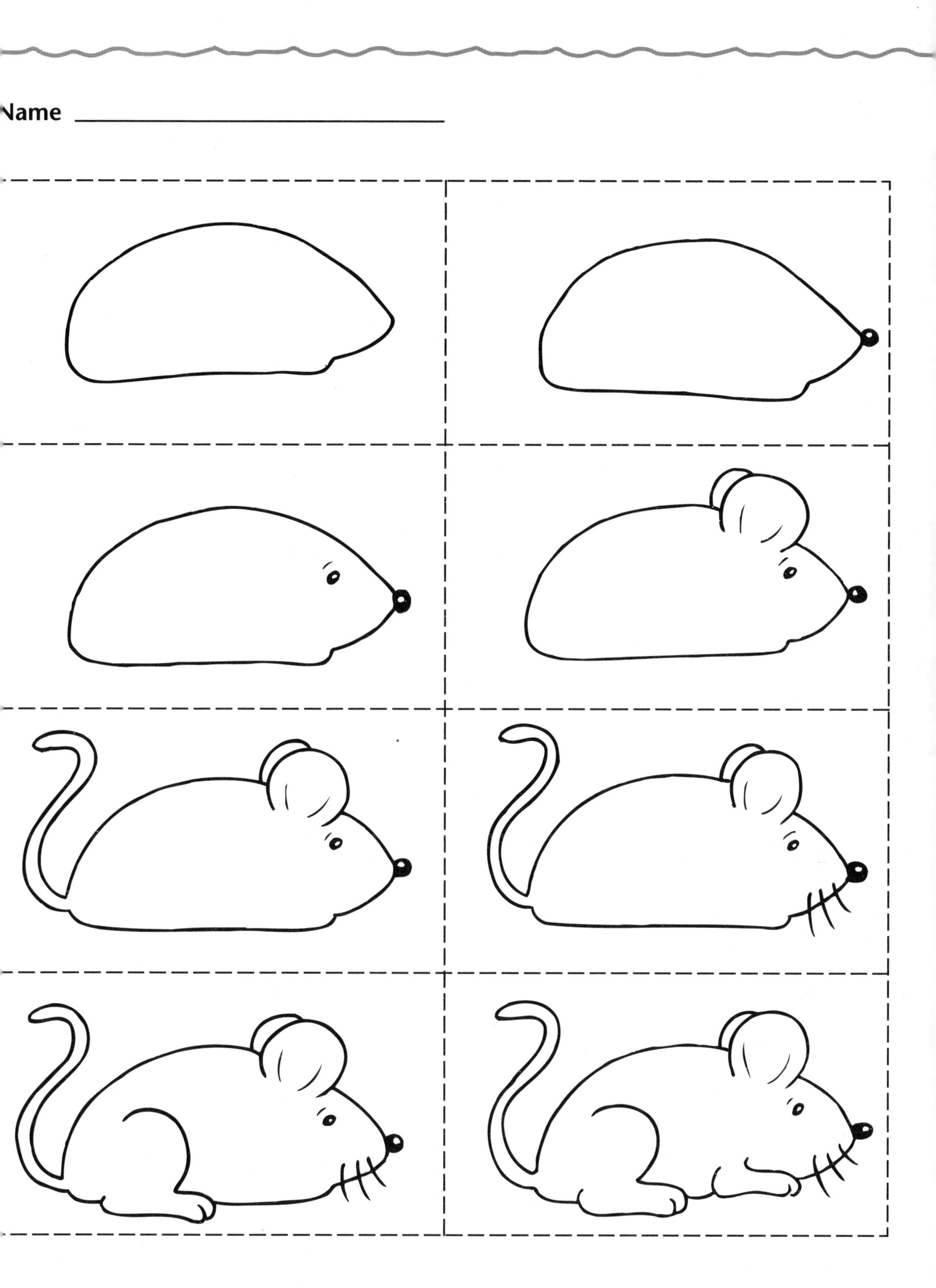

Name ______________________________

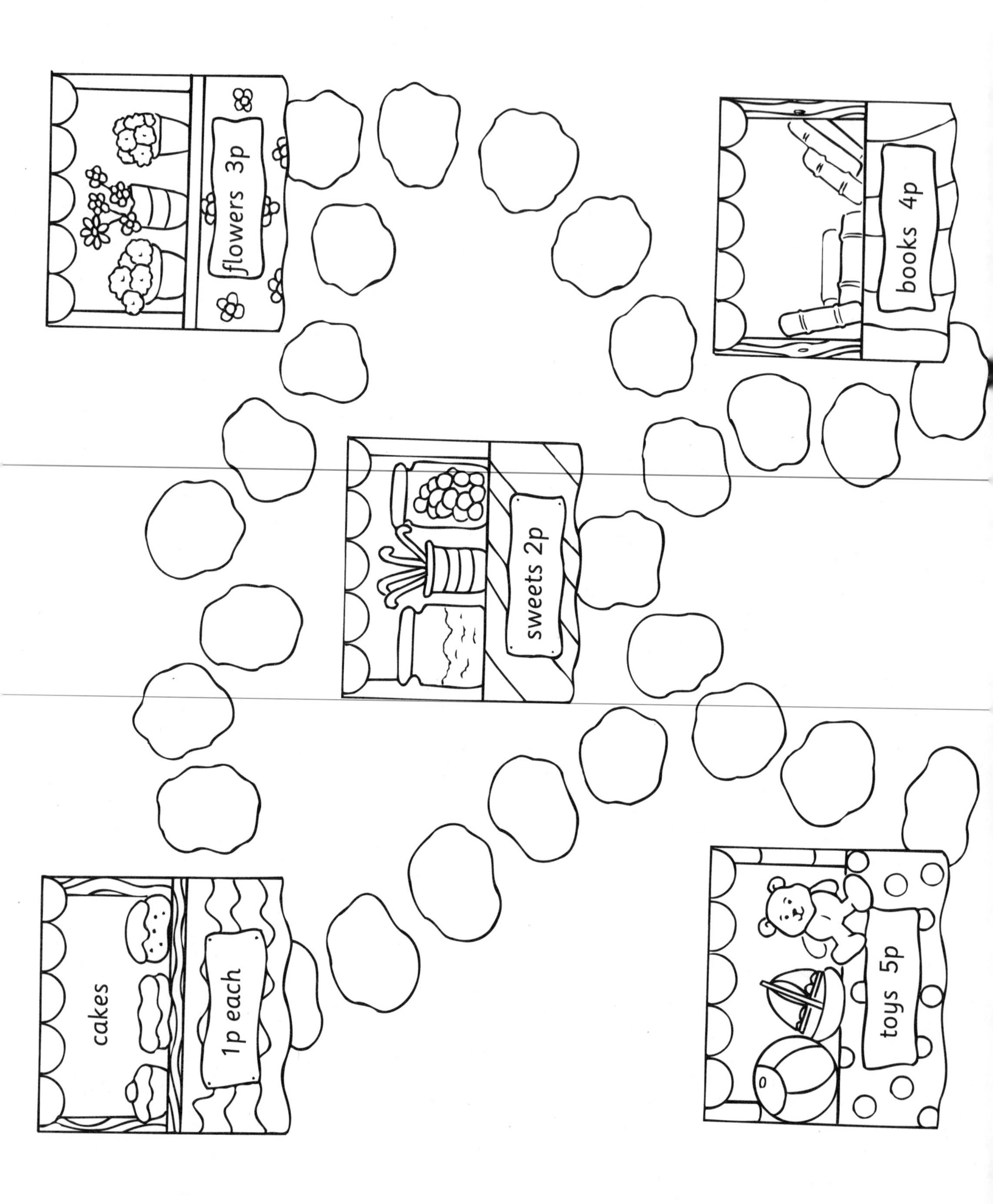

Name ______________________________

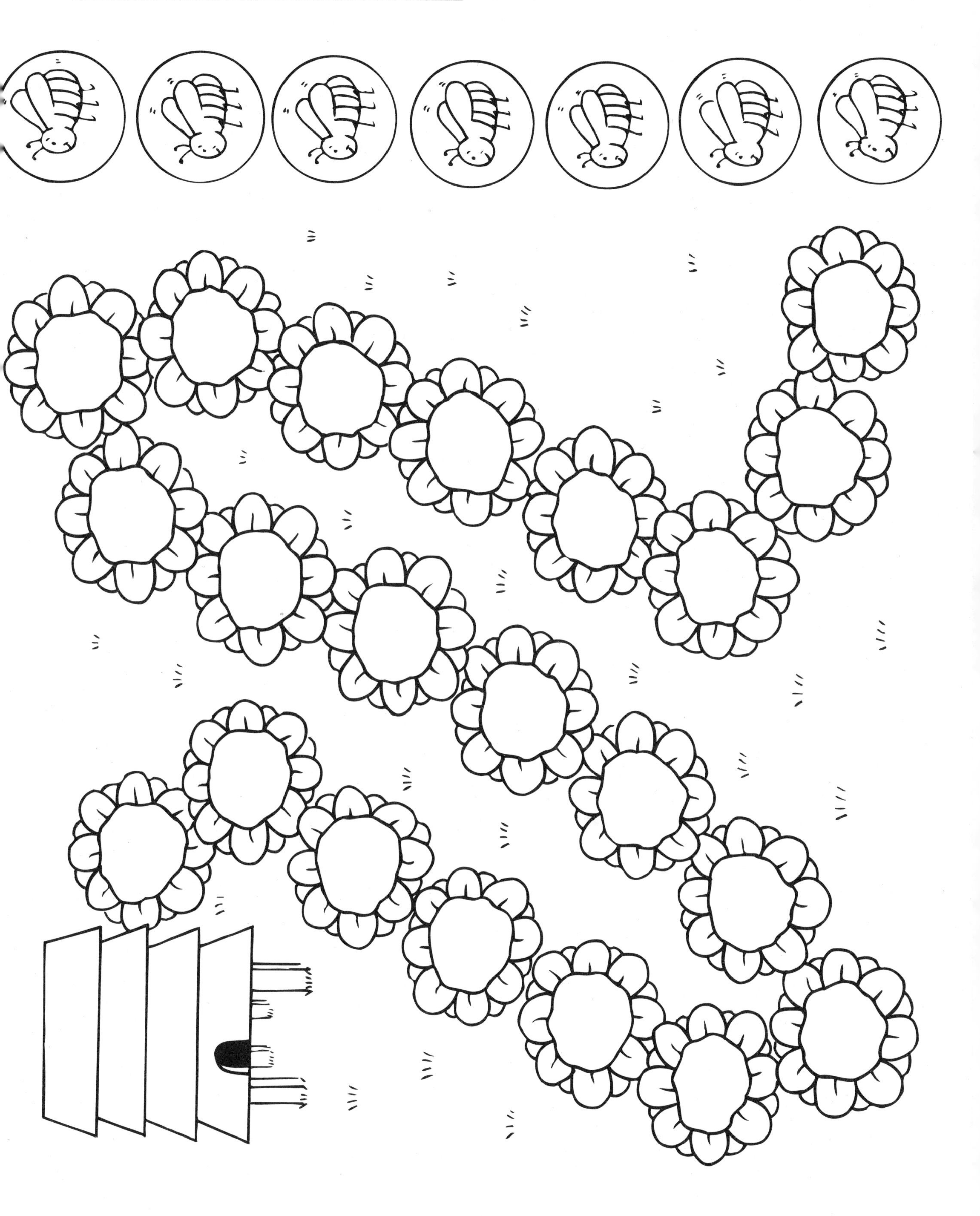

Name ______________________